Being You

A body and soul guide from the hearts of Irish women

Suzanne Power

BEING YOU

First published in 1996 by
HERO BOOKS LIMITED
50 City Quay, Dublin 2, Republic of Ireland.

ISBN No. 0 9526260 1 2

The opinions expressed are those of the women interviewed and not necessarily those of the author. Some names have been changed to protect the identities of those who wished to remain anonymous.

Origination: Title Media Limited, Dublin
Printing: Colorprint, Dublin

Being You

A body and soul guide from
the hearts of Irish women

Dedication

For the women who shared their tears, laughter, pain, joy, experience and secrets with me.
And for Michael who helps me to share mine.

THANKS TO...

Anna Meegan, who gave me the benefit of her caring and expertise in putting the concept together.

Jacqueline Traynor, my good friend and editorial assistant who created order out of chaos, generated enthusiasm and encouragement when mine had wilted and convinced me I could do it.

The women of Ringsend Community Centre and Cherry Orchard Family Resource Centre for some very powerful and funny moments.

Judith Ashton, Magdalen Bristow, Rosemary Khalifa, Marie Murray and Margaret O'Riordan for their encouragement, support and wonderful ideas.

Judith Crowe for her thoughts and extensive professional insight on preparation for motherhood.

Joyce Rowe for her thoughts on the same and for putting me in touch with interviewees.

Bridann Reidy for helping me to understand the true meaning of assertion and personal power.

Ailbhe Smith of the Women's Education and Resource Centre, Anne Marie MacMahon and Orla O'Neill of the Dublin Stress Clinic and Peadar O'Grady for their knowledge and guidance in their individual areas of expertise.

Dr Patrick McKeon, Chairman of AWARE.

Chubb for technical support, three square meals and neck rubs.

Siobhain MacNally and Mary Lucas for their much appreciated help with transcription and feedback.

Catherine O'Dea and Noeleen Slattery for their listening ears.

Eva Byrne, fabulous illustrator, fabulous woman.

Finally the warmest thanks to everyone at the Title Media Group who worked on this project. Especially Gwendoline Begley, a talented creature and a soothing voice at times when the stress needle shot into the red zone, and Marianne Hartigan, the editor.

Cathal and Liam, for having the belief and commitment to commission me in the first place.

And Liz and Anne, for telling them what a good idea it was to ask women what they think.

— *Suzanne Power, November 1996*

Contents

HELLO

THE IDEA FOR *Being You* has been around for some time — but really came into being at an Un-Valentine's Day party celebrated with friends in February this year. I felt very much part of the warm, confiding, enlightening atmosphere that makes female friendship so special. I realised I had learned more about relationships and Irish women's experiences of them that evening than I ever did reading books along the lines of *Get the Best Out of Your Lover* or *Stand on Your Head and Do It Right Now.*

These books are like express trains. If you're strong enough to hang on until the end then you stand a good chance of achieving something important. If you're not ready, feel uncertain, lack self-esteem, have no support system and feel powerless then you'll probably fall off after Chapter Three.

Irish women from ordinary backgrounds leading ordinary lives can be left feeling overwhelmed by the tidal wave of internationally renowned formula sellers who sweep through the country on an annual basis delivering their messages in select function rooms for £25 a head, plus lunch. Their ideas are inspiring if you can afford them and if you can memorise them on the day.

It takes significantly longer to work on personal growth and discovery, to develop self-esteem and confidence, to acknowledge our dreams — however big or small — and find the courage to start fulfilling them.

Who are the women who support us on a day-to-day basis? The women who will always be there at the end of the phone? The women who acknowledge our achievements and hold our hands when we fail?

Our friends and confidantes. Other Irish women. Women like us.

As women are very good at realising, there is no single right or wrong way to solve a problem. There are many approaches to it.

When a woman needs advice she will turn to those close to her and ask them what they think. If a woman lives in an isolated situation and does not have confidantes to discuss things with, she can avail of the directory in the back of the book to find out the relevant women's groups in her locality. Don't be afraid of getting in touch, many of the women involved with groups will have felt the same as you and will understand implicitly your fears and worries.

I got so much from Un-Valentines Day that it made me think. What if women all over the country were invited to give their accounts of the various hurdles, events and hoops they have faced in their lives? What about setting aside the "Ten Steps to the Tremendous New You" formulas and just do it our own way, the Irish way?

There is no typical Irish woman. According to the most recent figures there are 1,823,439 of us.

— 700,800 are or have been married.
— 149,800 are widowed
— 464,000 are single.
— 592, 771 have devoted our lives to bringing up our families.
— 454, 800 are part of the work force

They are the bare statistics. Every one of them is an individual with something unique and valuable to offer. But there are certain national characteristics which make us Females-On-The-Fringe-Of-Europe recognisable abroad. We tend to talk, we tend to have a great sense of family, it takes a while to know us but we make very good friends, many of us aren't as confident as we could be, we love a party and we are happier when we are surrounded by down-to-earth people.

We find the American method of analysing ourselves into a stew a bit much, we are still not as well paid and supported by society as most of our continental counterparts, but we seem to have a lot more fun. We view ourselves, in many ways, as the unequal, undervalued, 50% of the population. We are part of a very strict class system that can make us feel undermined and pigeon-holed.

What is Being You?

This is not a Self-Help book, this is an Everyone-Help book. The real-life experiences of women aged "15-going-on-16 to 70-something" provide the inspiration within these covers.

This is a book by Irish women for Irish women and also the men that love us and want to understand us better. It is a unique chance to hear our voices expressing a whole range of emotions and experience. It is a window into our world where we talk in loving as well as hurt and angry tones. You'll also get an insight into the things we often don't talk about too.

Being You is not written by doctors and experts and it is not based on scientific data or research, although they have been referred to and have contributed valuable advice. There are plenty of medical and psychiatric books on bookshelves to give you indepth analysis of each issue discussed in the various chapters. Please consult the reading lists at the end of each chapter for further reading.

Being You dips a toe in the water of women's issues and will provide you with a taste of what you can expect if you explore the issues further on your path of self-discovery. Some women have requested their names be changed in order to protect their identities. I have done so. The women who have contributed will not lay claim to leading perfect lives. But in at least one aspect of their existence they have done something exceptional and they share those experiences in order to help others going through it

They do not ask you to accept their choices as a model for your own existence, or a perfect formula.

They do not ask you to swallow what they say hook, line and sinker.

They do not ask you to follow what they say to the letter.

They do not ask you to change your life when you find it very difficult to change your circumstances.

They ask you just to be yourself — to enjoy the freedom of expression that brings — and they wish you all the best.

Chapter One

~~~~~~

BEING YOU

"When young... everything is a dress rehearsal... To be put right when the curtain goes up in earnest. Then one day you know the curtain was up all the time. That was the performance."
— **SYBILLE BEDFORD**, Meditations for Writers, Harper Collins.

Taking control of your life

WE LIVE IN AN ERA IN WHICH it is more possible than ever to be ourselves. To discover and develop in ways that our grandmothers never even dreamed of. Thanks to the generations of women who went before us, and to our own efforts, women in this country have come a long way and are continuing to break new boundaries.

Being You might seem an inordinate task when you don't even know who "you" are. It might seem very simple. It's as simple or as hard as you find it. Being true to yourself is the single biggest challenge in life, so it's bound to carry with it the greatest fears. All over the country there are people sitting at desks they don't want to sit at, doing jobs they don't want to do, saying things they don't really mean, living in places they don't like and being with people who get up their nose.

Women it seems are especially brilliant at this. We should all have degrees in the big A. Accommodation of others before ourselves.

Putting others first

MARGARET, 45: "I lived my life by the guiding principle that as soon as I got away from my mother... as soon as I got married... as soon as I finished rearing my children... as soon as the house was paid for... as soon as the dishes were washed... the ironing done... the husband's dinner cooked... — I would find time for myself. I am still waiting to find it."

Being busy can be very lonely. You rush around, over-extending yourself because it seems to be the only way to live life and the only way to get things done. You could be happy being busy or you could be running away — from yourself.

Deciding who you are and what you want to do is tricky. The reality is that everything you learn about yourself and do for yourself, is despite and because of, one key emotion — fear. Fear makes success taste like Belgian chocolate. In deciding who you are, you experience setbacks, failure, frustration, tears, indecision. Then the box of chocs arrives when you least expect it. Once you start letting yourself just be, you experience such energy you could take Sonia O'Sullivan on in Santry Stadium and give her a good run for her money.

Susan Jeffers, author of *Feel the Fear and Do It Anyway*, says:

> "At the bottom of every one of your fears is simply the fear you can't handle whatever life may bring you."

But we have a head start in that game — women are born handlers. We cope, we adapt, we react. We just have to get around the notion of putting ourselves first.

Self-esteem and being you

One of our basic rights as human beings is the right to self esteem. **SHARON CROWLEY** of Women Unlimited, runs courses in everything from stress management to quality of life on a budget. She believes self-esteem is a vital part of Being You — so what is it and how do you get it?

SHARON: "Self-esteem is basically what you think about yourself. You carry messages in your mind and heart, from those who have influenced your life. If they're good messages you tend to have high self-esteem, if they're bad messages you tend to have low self-esteem.

"Discovering yourself is largely about improving your self-esteem — discovering who you are and where you want to go. If your self-esteem is low you're not going to have the power to do the things you need to do with your life, to relax and live the life you want. You have to start with yourself. Believe you are a fabulous person — because you are. There is no-one else like you and there will never be anyone like you again."

FIONA, 39, has chosen to run her home and bring up her family. The decision required a lot of serious thought and lot of self-esteem because, although she has no doubt it was the right thing for her and her family, she feels called into question because of it:

> "I have been delighted to stay at home — and let me add immediately I don't think you need to stay at home to be a good mother. I want to give my children something which I consider to be invaluable — self-esteem. Something I have myself. But, being third-level educated you're caught in the dilemma that if you choose to stay at home, you are perceived as not taking advantage of the education that you have been given.
>
> "It can be very annoying to see some people's reaction because I feel I made a choice which was very valuable to society. I'm sure there are plenty of other women who would like to do the same if only they had the opportunity.
>
> "I've got the right to choose to stay at home because I have a partner who earns enough to keep both of us. That's a huge advantage — less and less people are in that position now. I won't pay lip service to the women who don't have my advantages in life but I will say this — you have the right to do whatever you want to do.
>
> "Just because I don't go out to earn a living does not mean I don't earn a living in my home. I'm worth my weight in gold and I know it. But I am lucky in that my parents instilled my self-worth into me and I have the self-esteem to cope with criticism. Women like me, who do a lot of different jobs within the home, at times feel under pressure because theirs is not a perceived career or perceived earning job. I justify it at times — I say 'I do this and this' etc. Intellectually this is foolish, but you come under pressure from society.
>
> "I get caught between wanting to support my husband in the best way I can by being here and taking care of the domestic burdens, then feeling at times society's lack of approval and lack of appreciation, because what I do is not seen — tidying up, putting the food on the table, putting on a wash. It's constant background stuff."

Society says your value is equated to whatever money you earn. So if you're unemployed, you're not very valuable, if you're a non-earning partner, you're not very valuable. Basing people's worth on pieces of paper generated from the Central Bank is giving them a false notion of themselves — the ones with lots of paper can think they're better than everyone else. The ones with very little paper can be made to feel they're worth nothing, particularly if they have not done a lot of personal growth work in their lives.

Here are two women who have seen beyond all that.

MAGDALEN BRISTOW, runs workshops for women on health issues, she is a trained nurse and an inspiration to talk to. Her life experience and vocation has led her to believe one thing above everything else. Women have a lot to offer, they are resilient and caring:

> "I feel for a lot of women — working women especially. It's as if they're on a permanent double shift system, out at work all day, then into childminding, meal making and housework in the evening.
>
> "One essential thing for them to realise is poverty does not mean misery — my father died when we were very young and my mother brought us up alone — six of us. She called me in one day from playing and I thought I'd had it. But she put her arms around me and pulled on a hat she had knitted for me, saying: 'Good people are very precious'.

It has stayed with me all my life and whenever I am in a difficult situation I just put that hat on and feel better."

MARIE, 27, grew up in a house where money was no object:

"At Christmas in our house we had half of Roches Stores under the tree. We had one of the first videos in Ireland, the first this, the first that. When I got pregnant at 19, at college, my parents cut me off. I had to survive with nothing. One of my friends ran a farm and he gave me a bag of vegetables each week. Myself and my daughter lived on those vegetables and very little else. When I sent letters to my family asking for money they thought I was joking.

"Well I survived! My daughter survived! Without their money! We had friends around us who supported us with their spirit when they had nothing else to give.

"I really know what it means to go hungry, I know what it means to have nothing. But I have gained so much I would never want to go back to the days of stuffed wardrobes and plenty of toys. I have all the best things now.

"Of course it is not all good. When my daughter does not get roller blades for her birthday and every other kid has them I feel sick. But she doesn't seem to mind half as much as I do. We have a lot.

"Someday I would like to be in the position to feel financially secure. But I do not base my life on money any more. I can't be bought and neither can my daughter."

Following your dreams

For the purposes of this book I surveyed many women and asked them what they would do with their lives if they won the Lotto. The answers they gave, the real answers after the cars, boats, holidays, new houses and gifts, had very little to do with money. Here are a few choice examples:

"I'd move to the country." — Well maybe you can do it anyway? There are plenty of country places within commuting distance of cities. If you live in council accommodation you can always apply to the Rural Resettlement Programme to relocate.

"I'd travel the world and see all the places I've only ever dreamed about." The biggest group of world travellers are students and young people. They work their way from country to country and enjoy their travels all the more for getting to know a few people who actually live there instead of other visitors hot-footing to the tourist attractions.

"I'd give up my job and retrain as something else." There are women studying all over this country. They manage to work and run homes too.

"I'd help my family." Like Marie, you probably already are giving them something more valuable than money — love and understanding, support and caring.

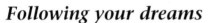

What all the wishes had in common was an

element of risk. Many women are frightened of taking risks. Maybe because the risks are frightening. It's very common for those of us with self-esteem the size of a small peanut to feel incapable of taking them. Self-esteem has not as much to do with big jobs and financial security as you might think. It can make you feel more secure to have a few bob in the bank of course — no one is denying that. But the deeply annoying thing is if you were to win a million it would only buy some of your dreams. Self-esteem will give you the confidence to chase others.

Louise, 21:

> "I hate myself. I'm only interested in one thing in life — sport. I was crap at school and only did one year after the Group Cert. I hated it. I'm not qualified to do anything so I've ended up working in a factory. I hate the boredom of the production line. I hate being indoors all day. My parents are threatening to kick me out because I'm so hyper. I hate my life. They all tell me I should get onto a sports' course but I know I'd never get that. I want it too much."

I got the above answer, in reply to the question: "How much are you worth in your opinion?" Isn't it alarming to see the word "hate" five times in one paragraph? Louise feels powerless in her own existence — destined for a life not of her own choosing because she does not think she's worth anything else. But by expanding so much on the question she probably wants help. How many of us have felt like that at some stage in our lives?

You've a tall order on your hands if you expect to achieve anything carrying that amount of pressure on your shoulders. The sense of isolation, the hurt, the depression and the lack of sympathy from others who are just browned off listening to your moans can make you feel even going to the shops is an insurmountable task.

EXERCISE

What makes you unhappy?

Let's get rid of the one tonne weight sitting on your head. Here's something for you. Take a piece of paper and write this heading across the top:

LICENCE TO MOAN

ISSUE DATE:................................You choose

EXPIRY DATE: ....Whenever
INSTRUCTIONS: Write down every single whinge, whine, bitch, miaow, grumble, grouse, grouch, explosion, complaint, carp, injustice.

   Take as long as you like over it, fill a copybook, fill a page, let everything negative pour out. If you feel you're no good at writing use single words.

Cry, sob, whimper, sniffle, snivel, shout over them. Do what you have to do. Fold this licence up and stick it in an envelope, seal it. Come back to it after a significant period of time and see how much of it is relevant to you now. The fears still present are the ones that you will need to seek advice on. But for now try not to show it to anyone else. There are things on this list you will laugh at in a month's time. Besides for the moment you don't need anyone to feel sorry for you, because this licence has the following:

ENTITLEMENTS:
Permission to feel as sorry for yourself as you like. You are worth feeling sorry for.
Permission to come back and add to the list.
Permission to do something nice for yourself every time something rotten happens to you.
Permission to stay *exactly* as you are if you don't feel like tackling any of the things on your list until such times as you do.

A problem shared....

Once you've reviewed your list it might be helpful to communicate the fears still present to someone who cares about you. Do this at a time when you feel you can express what you're going through. For example it would not be helpful if you told your man how miserable you are just after accusing him of eyeing up another women. It's not productive to reveal your inner despair to your mother just after you've told her how she never hugged you. And your best friend will not want to hear about your troubles when you've screamed like a banshee about how you're fed up listening to her.

Now you've written your negative thoughts on paper, imagine you can put it to one side and not feel any of those fears when you try this exercise. You'll need another blank sheet of paper:

LICENCE TO DREAM

DATE OF ISSUE: Now.
EXPIRY DATE: Whenever all the objectives
are achieved. Roughly when you take your last breath.
INSTRUCTIONS: Place all your secret and public desires
and wants on paper. Number them all in order of importance and Do-Ability.
Look at the finished list. Decide which one is easiest to
achieve and write out the steps you need to do it.
EXAMPLE: I've always wanted to learn a foreign language,
or improve my Irish.

Think about how impossible that is — then think about the possibilities. There are no classes in the area, so put a small advert in the paper and see if anyone else is interested in setting one up. There might be a foreign student or an Irish speaker willing to help with a conversation group in return for something else. Try and take all the possibilities into consideration. Your dreams can be trans-lated into reality if you take a step-by-step approach. If you want to skydive you don't leap out of a plane without a parachute because you can't afford one. You look for ways of borrowing a parachute.

ENTITLEMENTS:

Permission to take as long as you need fulfilling even the simplest dream. Life lasts a long time.
Permission to concentrate on the steps rather than the goal if you are afraid you won't get there. Each step taken is something achieved.
Permission to appreciate your efforts and remember the means are just as important as the end.

Fitting in

These exercises can help you sort out the first steps to finding out who you are and what you want to be. But another huge concern for us is that once we start this rollercoaster we will not find the stop button. What if we decide we hate our job? What if we don't like the people we've been socialising with? What if?... We could be here all day listing the "What Ifs?" but they all lead to the same worry:

What if I don't fit in?

The fear of not fitting in can be significant in your approach to life.

JULIE, 34: "I find myself doing stupid things just to be liked. Taking on too much to impress, agreeing with things I don't want to agree with. When I meet someone new I find myself adapting their mannerisms. It's like I'm afraid to be who I am."

If we're honest that will strike a chord with many of us.

NOREEN, 53 has found her answer to be herself, by recognising the fact she does not fit in anywhere in particular, and does not have to fit in:

"No. I don't fit in anywhere I feel. I know my friends and my loved ones would be really upset, but no matter where I go I don't really fit in. Being working class I kind of envy the middle classes. At a social event everyone seems to feel entirely comfortable, and I really envy that.

"I have to struggle to be happy in two worlds. I have a very strong sense of family. I still struggle to maintain that sense of family and where I'm from and that really means more to me than belonging to any particular social grouping.

"But I do have a real sense of myself. I suppose I started off with politics, reading political books and history, then moving on to personal and self-development and health issues. When I was younger I needed to cause a row in order to get my needs met. I couldn't say, as a man would, 'I am going to play golf on Wednesday afternoon', if I wanted to create space for myself, I would have to start a row in order to get out.

"Realising that led me on to say 'I am a human being, just say what I want'."

Education — the door opener

A little knowledge goes a long way. So **SARAH**, 26, realised when her local family resource centre, in Cherry Orchard, Co. Dublin, invited her to attend a University Awareness Week:

"It seemed to me that university was the domain of rich people with a few thousand quid to spare. I could not believe it when the speakers, all teachers and lecturers, spoke about their own backgrounds. Most of them had left school at 13, gone back as mature students to study and ended up teaching their subjects.

"As a result of meeting them I am doing a correspondence Montessori course and courses in Communications and Business Studies. I will set up my own school when I have finished.

"Everyone has the right to an education. My mother just got her Leaving Cert English. People in my area are going back to school after years on the dole. I used to feel trapped, frustrated, living with a husband and three kids in an area I didn't know. Now I feel like doors are opening all over the place. I am not afraid anymore to disagree with what someone says. I am not afraid to leave a situation I am uncomfortable with. I have discovered me.

"This has happened through a lot of things. But my writing especially has opened up my life. I used to scribble as a child when we went on holidays to a caravan. There was no television so I would read out what I had written to my cousins at the end of each day. If I did not have the story finished by the end of the holiday there would be hell to pay.

"I have come back to writing in the last two years. Three of my plays have been staged by various women's groups in the city centre and Ballyfermot.

"I'm like a snake. I've shed an old skin and underneath I find a new one. The real me. I like who I am. I just wish every woman could feel the same way. Don't let yourself get defeated by the hardship and misunderstanding all around you. We all feel the same way. Just go for it. Talk to your friends, make friends by joining groups, look for help in your community. You can find a way through. "

THE BEING YOU CHALLENGE

Your answers to these questions will give you an insight into your current state of mind and whether you want to look for the person inside you.

DO I SPEND ANY TIME WITH MYSELF WITH NO DISTRAC-
TIONS?
AM I UNCOMFORTABLE WITH SILENCE?
HOW DO I FEEL OTHER PEOPLE SEE ME?
WHAT STANDS IN THE WAY OF MY LIFE?
HOW MANY PEOPLE CONFIDE THEIR PROBLEMS IN ME?
WHAT HAVE I ACHIEVED SO FAR THAT I AM PROUD OF?
HOW MANY PEOPLE CAN I CONFIDE IN?
DOES MY PARTNER REALISE WHO I AM?
DO I REALISE WHO I AM?
HOW MUCH WAS I ENCOURAGED AS A CHILD?
WHO ENCOURAGES ME NOW?
WHEN WAS THE LAST TIME I LAUGHED OUT LOUD?
AM I APPRECIATED?
DO I GET TO DO SOMETHING I LIKE EVERY DAY?

Analyse your answers, try to broaden your mind to include options which might bring about positive answers to the questions. Add to the list with questions of your own that you want answered. They are the most important ones of all.

FURTHER READING
A Woman In Your Own Right
By Anne Dickson
Quartet Books

The Mirror Within
By Anne Dickson
Quartet Books

Our Bodies Ourselves
By Angela Dickson and Jill Rakusen
Penguin

Feel the Fear and Do It Anyway
By Susan Jeffers
Arrow Books

The Road Less Travelled
By M. Scott Peck
Arrow Books

Meditations for Women Who do Too Much
By Anne Wilson Schaef
Harper Collins

Self Esteem

Personal Development

Assertiveness

Chapter Two

~~~~~~

FINDING YOU

PERSONAL DEVELOPMENT and assertiveness are two of the most valuable aspects of self exploration and progress in anyone's life. The more time we spend rushing around the less time we spend thinking about ourselves in each situation. The courses run in personal development and assertiveness nationwide give women a chance to take time out, 'Me Time', to look first at themselves, then at their approach to life and dealings with others, to equip them better to deal with a world of high expectations within short time frames.

This chapter focuses on the four central issues involved in learning how to find out who you are and what you want out of life. First you need to deal with your own personal issues; then focus on learning how to communicate with people assertively; add to this the ability to say 'No' without fear of letting loved ones down; and finally look at personal empowerment.

Personal development

Because we tend to spend more time focusing on others, without really having the opportunity to look at ourselves, many women interested in assertiveness end up doing personal development work first, before moving onto an assertiveness course. New Opportunities for Women (NOW), a European Social Fund initiative, has made a lot of inroads into this area on a nationwide basis.

Apart from going through the traditional routes to improve your self-esteem and assertiveness skills, the Outdoors NOW project was funded by the National Youth Council and the NOW programme to promote personal development through physical activities and strategy. Rising to physical challenges creates a real sense of achievement and enhances relaxation.

Women don't have as much access to sport and sporting facilities as men. If you go down through the list of sports clubs in your locality the chances are most of them will be male dominated: football, hurling, rugby, golf... It seems unfair when you consider our two most prominent sporting achievers in recent years have been women. We can't all be Sonias and Michelles, but we can all get the benefit of working our bodies for own Personal Best.

MARGARET, 24, is one woman who has discovered this for herself through the Outdoors NOW courses:

"I found out about the outward bound course through a notice in my community centre. I had no-one to go with so I went on my own. The other women all made me feel very welcome so I didn't feel out of place. The hardest thing was abseiling down a cliff. It wasn't that high but I get dizzy standing on a chair. I did it, thanks to the encouragement of my instructor and the other women. I dangled at the edge for ages, which is the worst thing you can do.

"One of the instructors told me to look into her eyes and just lean back. It worked. I dribbled down like a snail but I did it. There was a big cheer when I hit the ground and the rush of adrenaline raced through me. I was sky high all the rest of the day.

"It did wonders for my self-esteem and confidence. I believe outdoor pursuits can make you more rounded as an individual. Women need to have more access to them. I'm from a rural area and I never would have really used the countryside around me. Rising to physical challenges helps you to rise to the internal ones."

The courses have now finished but a club has formed which organises regular outdoor activities. Contact Nora Sweetman on 5 Tritonville Ave, Sandymount, Dublin 4, or contact the National Youth Council.

For couch potatoes and those of us who might want to work their grey muscle first before taking up any physical activities — don't worry — you don't necessarily have to scramble up mountain-sides to find yourself. Many women have gone to their local adult education or resource centre to take personal development courses. Many have found it to be the most positive step they have taken in their lives so far:

EILEEN, 38, did a personal development course and found it opened not only her eyes, but those of her family.

"What you get from a personal development course you would not get from winning the Lotto. Before I came to do one I would never have talked about myself, my problems. When I look at my husband and children they have gained a lot from me doing it too. My little fella said to me only a couple of weeks ago, 'You have no listening skills!' Because he was not getting my attention about something. When I asked my eldest girl to go clean her room and take the look off her face she said 'I'm only establishing eye contact Mammy!'

"I've stuck a bill of rights to the fridge and my kids will tell you their rights now. I feel through the course I'm no-one's mother, no-one's lover, I'm just me and that course was a place where I could just be.

"I never used to cry. I was never one for showing my feelings. Every week of the course, practically, I cried. You could just tell that group anything. I felt very much hard done by, but now I see that each situation is what you make of it. People are just so threatened by the work you do on yourself. Your family and friends see somebody different coming out of it. But it helps them grow too.

"For the first two weeks of the course everyone is starting to get to know one another. There is a lot of tension in the room because you don't want to reveal anything. You spend most of your life putting on a brave face and then you are suddenly given the permission to talk about the things that are going on, to get to know yourself. It made me face reality."

One of the chief rewards is the level of intimacy which can spring up among women, like **JOANNE, MONICA** and **SARAH,** working towards personal goals and insights:

JOANNE, 27: "It's amazing really. When you get a group of women together to do this kind of work and sharing, you can never go back to just saying 'Howaya?' to each other. You need to know how they really are."

MONICA, 37: "Before working on my personal development I never really trusted anybody. I mean, nobody is supposed to know your business and that's it. Don't tell anyone how you feel, your feelings don't mean anything. It's very lonely.

"For a long time I hid behind drink, because I grew up with a father who was very fond of it and, in order for me to hide from the things that were going on, I went on a similar road.

"Through personal development I discovered that was not for me. I was taking his path instead of taking my own and doing my own thing. Personal development stops the pain. To me it opened a door to realise how much I am a person. You get it into your head that this is the way things are supposed to go on and there is no other road. You say you have survived up to now, but it's no good surviving unless you survive for you — not just for the sake of it.

"If you said to me, six years ago, that I was going to sit in this room and tell this person, with a tape recorder, what I grew up with, I'd have said no way.

"Now I'm here, talking to you. I have my own life and way of looking at things. That's what it did for me."

SARAH, 26: "I have been very hard on myself but every week, after the personal development course, I went out that door feeling easier and easier about myself and my life. You are not the same person after it. It's the foundation for everything — before you can go on with life. It gives you that enthusiasm, that sense of being a great woman. It's not just the family anymore, it's yourself and you can come up to the course and have a break and make friends and all of those important things."

If personal development sets the ball rolling, assertiveness takes things a step further. It gives you the courage and skills to look at the future, develop a vision for yourself and what you will become in the years ahead. Most of us will be assertive in some areas of our life but it is very rare to find someone who is assertive in every aspect of her existence. A big hurdle is learning how to fulfill our own needs before, and as well as, those of the people we love and relate to.

Communication skills

A number of people equate assertiveness with being aggressive and getting your own way. It's actually the complete opposite. You are not assertive if you are pushy, arrogant and determined to get your own way at all costs.

The key to assertive behaviour lies in respecting the other person you're communicating with and communicating what you have to say in a way that respects their position.

You don't put yourself in a situation where you're going to be put down but equally you don't end up doing that to someone else. That's a core concept.

Assertiveness training offers you a valuable philosophy of life and set of skills very relevant to women's lives. There is no one way to become assertive, each situation is different.

Learning to express your feelings, including the thorny ones like anger, rejection and criticism, is an essential part. These three merit a book in themselves and within the confines of this chapter it would be impossible to give you a guide to managing them, except to suggest you read up further using the booklist at the end of the chapter and also start some sort of training in those areas.

Self disclosure

Self disclosure is being honest about how you feel when you're talking to somebody. This is not an admission of failure, it is a way of letting yourself feel more at ease with life. Actually saying: 'I feel anxious about bringing this up,' 'I feel awkward saying this' can be empowering.

To admit this is to start noticing how you feel. Once you start looking at you, and considering yourself in every situation, you are learning and practising assertion.

Apart from using self-disclosure, in an assertiveness class women learn to look at their own communication styles, particularly when dealing with difficult situations.

For now we will stick to the four, very general, ways in which we express ourselves with other human beings and receive feedback. In reality you will find you might approach individual situations in two or more of the manners described in the next few pages. We are complex creatures with complex behaviour patterns. To analyse them singly is to give you an insight into the path you take at any given moment, but really we are a combination of all these behaviour patterns.

AGGRESSIVE — We behave in a loud and forceful manner in order to drown out the other person's point of view. Many women would mistake this 'get out of my way or else' approach as being assertive. In fact it shows a lack of self-worth, because you're not really confident enough to take on board other people's point of view:

> **LORRAINE**, 24: "I am seen by a lot of people as tough, ready to take on the world and its mother. But, through assertiveness work, I have come to realise that railroading other people into doing what I want to do, or shouting others down is not the way to express myself. From an early age I was taught to win, even the bloody egg-and-spoon race at sports day. I used to run competitively and I felt it was never any good to finish second. It was first or not at all.
>
> "In college projects I would foist myself into the leadership role and tell my team exactly what they should do and how to do it. OK, we did well, but I didn't really realise how much resentment I created by not allowing other people have their say. I do still tend to shout my way to recognition, but I am trying very hard to listen to others now and not to be afraid of their initiative. Role play in the assertiveness course was important to me. I learned to like myself enough to let other people finish their sentences."

PASSIVE — Allowing others to determine the course of your life, from where you will go on Friday night, to when you get married or what you will do as a career. Making other people feel good by allowing them to run your show and running away from confrontation when you do. These are all characteristics of a passive person, someone not really in control of their own life.

ORLA, 30, did an assertiveness course 10 years ago because she felt she was too passive, particularly at work:

> "I was a sap, a doormat. From the first night of the course I felt I was learning how to deal with this. We discussed personality types, and situations where you would feel you are or aren't assertive. The role play was very enlightening. We would look at everyday situations, like: if somebody skips a queue, what do you do about it?
>
> "I found I could change my behaviour, because I was always doing things that I didn't want to do, going to places with people that I didn't want to. I couldn't say no. People-pleasing is no good because you never please yourself. If you believe in yourself as a person then you believe you have rights."

Women in an assertiveness group share how they're feeling in different situations. In our society you are supposed to be able to cope and if you express strong feelings by crying or getting angry it seems to mean you're not coping. So we try to hide and suppress those feelings. The amount of energy it takes to keep those feelings under wraps is extraordinary.

Orla felt unable to express her dissension or use her own voice to establish her identity, but now:

> "It's a gift to know I have the right to say 'I don't like that' or 'I don't want to go there'."

INDIRECTLY AGGRESSIVE — Women are often seen as mistresses of manipulation. In actual fact this again points to a lack of self esteem and worth. Some of us cannot risk the direct approach for fear of repercussions. Women are not generally encouraged to be direct, open and straightforward. Look at the trouble Lizzie had with high society in Pride and Prejudice. In some ways the social mores of the Austen era stand true today. Shooting from the hip is a hard thing to do if you're considered to be a member of the gentler, fairer sex.

Making others feel guilty can be a signal to yourself that you're acting with indirect aggression. How many times have we used this device to twist men around our little fingers?

NOELEEN, 46 saw herself doing this with her children and husband:

"My old war cry was 'Do I have to do everything around here?' And then I'd carry on doing it. My own mother was an expert on making you feel guilty and I felt shocked when I came to realise I did exactly the same things.

"If my husband was heading out to a game of football I would say: 'It's well you have the time to enjoy yourself, I might get out when I finish the housework.' Instead of saying, 'I'd like to spend more time with you and to get some more help around the house can we do that?'

"The two girls were always encouraged to be 'good'. I would never shout at them or hit them but I would make them feel guilty for making a show of me. I was a bit of a martyr.

"Now the dishes can sit in the sink all day. If they want to help they can help, if they don't I won't whine and wheedle. I get on with my own life and interests and they get on with theirs. It makes for a more peaceful life. I don't expect my children to lead the life I led, to take on the responsibilities I took on. They have their own lives to get on with. When I want co-operation I ask for it — straight out."

ASSERTIVE — When you learn to respect yourself and others you learn your life is your own. You set your own goals and don't try to impede others from theirs. You take initiative on the way you want to live. You recognise your needs and express them through direct communication. This enhances your self-esteem and confidence and gives you the courage to face the next sections — *Saying No and Personal Power*.

Remember — to recognise any of these characteristics in yourself is not an admission of failure. These are all very natural ways in which we respond when we find ourselves in tricky situations. Looking at your own communication style: passive, aggressive, indirectly aggressive or assertive — you begin to see there are ways in which you can deal with difficult situations that would be more effective.

If you are assertive you are communicating in a clear, direct, open and honest way, whether you're looking for help in dealing with your family, work or in a social context.

Saying 'No' and the compassion trap

"No" is such a simple, expressive, direct, vital word. But it seems to be the one women have a certain amount of difficulty in saying.

The physical instructions are easy to follow: stick your tongue against the roof of your mouth and exercise a few vocal chords, then round your lips into an O shape.

If only it were so simple.

Very often as women we have learned how to put other people first and as a result we have a poor sense of ourselves and a low sense of self worth. If we can recognise what is right for us in our lives, identify what we need and how we want our lives to be, this helps us to develop a strong sense of self. This in turn results in increased self-esteem.

Learning "No" is learning to set limits for yourself in your life and that is all about *Being You*. It's about deciding what is important, it's about deciding what kind of relationships you want to have with other people. From the time we are babies young girls are brought up to think of other people and focus on others. To begin to claim that focus back, to learn to think about yourself first, is hard.

Women beginning to use the word 'No' effectively think they have to start being selfish. This is not necessarily the case. A lot of the source of personal power and good mental health is to do with having a sense of yourself.

In Ireland we have all largely been brought up in the Catholic tradition. Lapsed or unlapsed there is still certain social conditioning around it. Good people are seen as selfless, willing to give, helpers, untiring, generous...

This is the Compassion Trap, out of feeding the needs of others we forget to feed ourselves.

JACKIE, 34, is one woman who recognised this in herself:

"I had the tendency to lean towards the word 'Yes'. No matter what anybody wanted me to do, I was always available. It made me feel sick with guilt if I refused something to anyone, no matter how small the favour.

"I got a great sense of well-being from the assertiveness course, I learned to say "No" some of the time.

"Through role play I came to deal with one situation in particular. I would be making the dinner and the phone would ring. It was always someone looking for an ear and I would give it to them. Ruined dinners were my reward for listening at the wrong time.

"The counsellor and group asked me how I would feel if the shoe was on the other foot and I was speaking to a friend that had no real interest in what I was saying. I decided I would not like it at all. It was so much easier to be honest with myself and my friends. I told them I would love to talk to them but I couldn't give them the attention they deserved at that moment. Then I would give them a definite time when I could ring back. Much less stress and frustration and I was being a better friend.

"Another thing was babysitting. Because I had only two kids and no outside work at the time I found myself a babysitting target. Early one morning a good friend called to ask if I would look after her four-week-old until one o'clock. I had plans to decorate. 4pm came and I had a screaming baby and two strips of wallpaper off the wall. I in turn had a screaming match with my friend.

"I was only harming myself, stressing myself out unneccessarily and not being a good friend at all. Through my assertiveness group I have learned the most useful word in the dictionary and family and friends know where they are with me. I help when I can and I am straight with them. I would recommend a course to anyone."

Personal empowerment, change and the bemused world

Taking your own path, making your own choices and dealing with the consequences of your own actions can give you tremendous personal power. But that kind of change can spark off a whole range of reactions in the people witnessing it. Particularly when they are not assertive themselves.

Suddenly you are not reacting in the way they're used to.

CLAIRE, 32, is a very successful marketing executive. She feels she benefited a great deal from doing an assertiveness course two years ago :

"I've always felt there were two me's. I'm very shy and I have learned to overcome that in a public situation by doing things like debating. So while I functioned well in the public domain, in a one-to-one situation, like job interviews, I was not quite as certain of my ground.

"One of the first topics we covered was expectations.

"Expectations about myself are fundamental to asserting who I am. I began to seriously think about that. I'm quite even tempered, a peace-maker. I like to keep everyone happy and my way of doing that is often to meet their expectations. When asked why, I realised it was because I wanted approval.

"This led me to my relationship with my parents, whom many would describe as perfect. But that in itself was a burden. My mother has enormous expectations of herself and I had to meet her standards. Also I am the eldest, which is a classic situation in itself. I was the one they experimented on.

"Most women of my generation would have had mothers who stayed at home all day long. Their big problem tends to be they suffer from guilt about not being at home with the kids. I suffer from the reverse. I feel guilty being at home and not at work.

"The Redwood assertiveness course, [which is the programme most of the interviewees chose to do] is about learning to like yourself. I really do like myself. I like the fact I have made a decision to have an interesting job at a level which allows me to enjoy my home life too."

Calling a halt to the 'Everyone Else Comes First' ethos can cause massive fallout: **LAURA**, 38:

"My mother hates me coming up to do personal development and assertiveness courses in my local adult education centre. She thinks I should be going over to her house and clearing it. An unpaid, domestic skivvy is what she wants and I'm just not prepared to be that anymore."

One of the toughest things about being an assertive female is you have to go through the conflict Laura is experiencing to come out the other side. It's part of the whole process of change and if you don't go through it you'll always be dependent on somebody's else's approval to do the things you need to do in your life.

Say: 'I'm doing this for myself' and 'I don't need other people's approval to do it.' Trust your own gut feeling that this is the right thing to do.

Women who start to change their behaviour and become assertive can get a hard time. People like things to stay the same and it is very threatening for others if women start doing things very differently.

CLAIRE, 32: "Depending on your circumstances you come up against some pretty difficult issues and problems through the assertiveness work. You end up doing some very serious talking to those close to you and in some instances you end up walking away from some people and things. I had to learn that part of being assertive was learning when to walk away. You just can't be responsible for the way others feel. You can't control them.
"You can't stay awake all night worrying about the people who are unhappy with you because you have become assertive. It's about learning not to expect other people's approval. To do it for your own sake and your own reasons."

Finding yourself in the "I am Who I Am" frame of mind allows you to break down another barrier facing many females.

Competition and comparison with other women

None of us like to think we do it, but I have my hand in the air, red-faced, as someone who has looked enviously at other women's figures (financial and physical), and futures. We do tend to compare ourselves to other women. This mightn't always lead on to competition and envy but it can.

Competing and comparing really eats away at your self-esteem.

But the good news is you don't have to compare, because you have the right to be different. You can have good and bad parts. You don't have to be like others. You don't need to see other people's achievements as a sign of your inadequacy.

It's difficult not to compete and compare because we are bombarded with images of how we are supposed to be — a particular shape, look a particular age, wear particular clothes and adopt particular roles.

JOANNE, 27: "I work in a very competitive industry. For years I found it hard to be pleased for women doing well in it, even friends. It all came down to me not feeling good enough. Now I work for myself it's much easier to be glad for the women I see doing well. I get inspiration from it. I think if they are doing well then I can do well."

If a woman is successful it doesn't mean you're inadequate. When we see a woman who is successful we often think it was easy for her to make it. Often it has been a struggle.

Comparing ourselves unfavourably with other women does not enhance self-esteem. We're wasting time and energy which could be spent motivating ourselves.

It's important that we support successful women in their achievements. Women forging ahead in visible ways can often be doing so at a personal cost to themselves. They are cutting a path for the rest of us.

Remember — from the start you are equal to others.

Learning assertion is about learning to communicate our needs and desires in a clear, direct, open and honest manner — in a way that does not put someone else down and equally does not allow us to be put down. It's about finding our own place.

You don't need to feel alone with your difficulties. As you can see from the women who've shared their experiences, there are plenty of others who feel the same as you do.

The final word must go to the woman responsible for helping thousands of Irish women stand up for themselves and their beliefs — Anne Dickson founded the Redwood Institute which trains women to become assertiveness trainers. In her book, *A Woman In Your Own Right*, she describes assertion as:

"Heart, mind and body work in unison — that is the moment of being personally power-ful."

EXERCISES

If you have a good friend or confidante ask them to work on these exercises with you. Discuss your dreams and findings with each other and support each other as you take a step in the right direction.

1. ASSERTIVENESS PLAN

For this you will need pen, paper, time and a good friend or family member. Sit down and write a list of all the things you want to do with yourself in the next 12 months. List each object in order of importance and the ease with which it can be achieved.

Once you have completed the list mull it over and decide on your first aim. Start with the easiest one. Decide which steps you will need to take to achieve it. Then work out a rough time span — realistically!

EXAMPLE:

1. I am going to learn how to drive.

STEP ONE: Apply for a provisional licence.

STEP TWO: Book a few lessons with a driving instructor.

STEP THREE: Enquire how much it will cost to get insurance as a learner...

Remember — each step is an achievement in itself. Ask for your friend's encouragement and provide her with the same back up.

2. SAYING "NO"

Get your exercise partner to ask you for simple things like the loan of a pen, a dress, a book. Then refuse their request politely and firmly. Don't list off a whole ream of reasons for your refusal, but do qualify your refusal with simple direct answers if it is questioned.

EXAMPLE:
"Can I borrow your book on meditation?"
"No."
'Why ever not?"
"Because I use it a lot for myself and I may need it when you have it. I can tell you where I bought it if you really want a copy..."

Discuss any difficulty in saying "No" you may have.

Further reading and information
BOOKS:
A Woman In Your Own Right
by Anne Dickson
Quartet Books

Our Bodies Ourselves
by Angela Phillips and Jill Rakunsen
Penguin

Fat is a Feminist Issue
by Susie Orbach
Hamlyn

Self Assertion for Women
by Pamela Butler
Harper and Row

For Ourselves
Anja Meulenbelt
Sheba

COURSES:
The Education Department, Well Woman Centre
Head Office, 73 Lower Leeson Street, Dublin 2. Ph 01- 661 0083

■ *Your local community resource centre or adult education centre will also know of courses.*

New Opportunities for Women
National Women's Council
32 Upper Fitzwilliam Street
Dublin 5
Contact: Mary Donnelly
Ph 01-661 5268

Outdoors NOW
c/o National Youth Council of Ireland
3 Montague Street
Dublin 2
Ph 01-478 4122

Irish Countrywomen's Association
58 Merrion Road
Dublin 4
Head office number: 01-668 4052/3

Chapter Three

~~~~~~

HOW OLD IS YOUR CAT?

Age and the Unclassified Woman

HOW OLD IS YOUR CAT? Who cares? How old are you? What does it matter? This chapter focuses on age and our perceptions of it. A few years ago I met a woman who was travelling alone through some of the most isolated, inaccessible parts of the world. Her name was Margaret and she was 67 years old. She had started to travel at 57, when her husband died and her family was reared. Before that she had never even left her native Australia.

Her travels were interrupted by two events: she lost an arm in a bus crash in Bombay and half a lung through cancer. As soon as she recovered she packed her rucksack and set off again. In the few days I spent with her in Pakistan, we trekked up hillsides and went white-water rafting on the Indus river. The Indus is no ordinary river. A documentary on rafting called it the Great White Lion, the most challenging stretch of water in the world. Our trip was pure terror in parts and my face showed it:

"The problem with young ones is they don't know how to let go, loosen up a bit!" she screeched as the torrential waters crashed in on us.

"What about you?" I replied, baling water out frantically. "At your age you might end up having a heart attack."

"At my age I'm young enough to appreciate the experience and old enough not to care what happens."

Back on dry land Margaret added this little gem:

"It's great to travel at my age. I wouldn't have had the sense to do it if I was any younger than 50."

It seems many of us feel trapped by our birth dates:

SARAH, 26: "I enjoyed being 18 best out of any age. I dislike being 26 because I have to be responsible a lot and I like to be a child sometimes."

GRAINNE, 33: "I dislike younger company alienating me because of my age. I am 23 in my soul and that was the age I packed a rucksack and slid out of the gene generating machine."

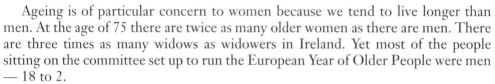

AMANDA, 21: "I hate the sex thing at this age, the way men aren't able to keep their hands off and cannot get their heads around committing for longer than a few dates."

MOLLY, 68: "I cannot get a thing to suit me in clothes shops which all seem to cater for younger women, they think I want to drink tea instead of whiskey and the doctor keeps telling me to give up things I love when it's at my time of life I can enjoy them most."

NELL, 57: "I don't think my husband thinks of me as a woman at all. I feel ugly and old at times. It seems the older I get the less affection I receive."

ROSEMARY, 32: "My body tells me I am in my 30s. My head says I'm around 13."

Ageing is of particular concern to women because we tend to live longer than men. At the age of 75 there are twice as many older women as there are men. There are three times as many widows as widowers in Ireland. Yet most of the people sitting on the committee set up to run the European Year of Older People were men — 18 to 2.

MAMO, 67, is Cathaoirleach of Age and Opportunity and the Older Women's Network, organisations dedicated to changing people's attitude towards ageing and older people, to promote positive images of ageing and to encourage greater participation on the part of older people and inter-generational solidarity.

They work through state, arts and sporting bodies to instill the philosophy of access and awareness for all ages:

"My grandson said to me when he visited recently 'You're not very wrinkly'. I said 'That's what comes from living in a house with no central heating. But I've just moved to a house where I do have it. I look forward and I am planning to become really wrinkly this winter'

"Life is what you make it, it doesn't have to be awful to get old. You might have to recognise certain physical limitations but there are other gifts which follow.

"The gift of time is most important. Time to take things more at your own pace. You wake up in the morning and the day is yours. You are not constrained by having to be at work at a certain time. I met a woman on the bus from Dublin to Monaghan recently. She told me on the first Monday after she retired she set the clock for the usual time just for the joy of switching it off and turning over to sleep again.

"At my age you also learn to have the freedom within yourself to say 'Yes I will do that' or 'No — I don't think I want to do that'. I hadn't the confidence to do so when I was younger. I was brought up in a very conformist time.

"I am enjoying growing old very, very much."

Ageing isn't confined to older people. You are ageing now. If you treat life as an adventure, exploring new possibilities and opportunities, you are going to have a fulfilled old age. But if you've stopped yourself doing things old age will bring frustration.

MAMO: "Some let life wash over them without doing anything to make life changes, but if you develop interests your age has less concern for you. It will help you enjoy your later years."

JENNIFER, 27: "Age is meaningless, maturity is what it is all about. I'm not being flippant but age has never been an issue with me. I often have to think about what age I am!"

That's a great attitude but she might find cause for reflection after looking through the 'situations vacant' columns. In most cases the advertisements are very specific in who they're looking for — right down to the age profile. Under 30 and you'll come keen and cheap. Under 35 and you're experienced, but with enough youth on your side to make you marketable. 35-50 and the jobs around are generally senior positions. Anything older than 50 and you're not likely to get a full time, pensionable position.

Unless you're **VANESSA**, 45 owner of 2nd Shift Recruitment Agency in Dublin:

"I have five children and spent 18 years in the home looking after them. It was extremely enjoyable but I had every intention of coming back into the work force.

"I knew it would be difficult — but I never realised how difficult. It hit me gradually — I was not wanted. I applied for so many jobs and followed up with so many phone calls. It was only a year or so ago I realised that if I was experiencing this difficulty so were others.

"I decided to set up my own recruitment agency which would not exclude mature people from the work force. In fact I would encourage them and fight to find jobs for them. To cut a long story short after a lot of sleepless nights trying to raise funding for start-up it happened. Needless to say I have been inundated with applications. So far my research — which discovered that the traditional age bias in putting experience to work, is actually creating a major gap in the employment market — has paid off.

"Employers need people who are reliable, they need people who are not going to flit off to another position after investing money training them and promoting them. They are gradually beginning to discover the need for older, experienced personnel who are loyal, reliable and dedicated.

"I'm not saying that younger people aren't but I think maturity brings something to a position that commands respect. Mature people are experienced people and our aim is to put that experience to work.

"The words NO AGE BARRIER appear on all our literature and advertisements. For many that is a message of hope. One man who came in here said 'I feel like I've been given a second chance.' We haven't even needed to advertise that heavily because the media has picked up on the concept and the public has got right behind us.

"People across the board come into us. Some are highly-skilled, easily placed workers. Others have been out of the work force for decades and genuinely believe they have nothing to offer, particularly if they are women. We're here to persuade them differently."

It takes people like Vanessa to make us realise how quickly we will dismiss good people as being "too old..." Too old for what? Too old for stunt acting, too old to run the country, too old to fall in love? No-one tells Anita Roddick or Moya Doherty to stop being successful because they're over 40 or that it's time to let a younger version take centre-stage. They're likely to laugh in the faces of those who try. No-one criticises 55-year old Susan Sarandon for loving the much younger Tim Robbins, or for looking so stunning on celluloid.

What these, and other women like them, do well is they ignore labels like age and get on with living. There are enough obstacles in their path without letting their lifestyle be dictated to them by the number of years they've been on the planet.

MARINA 49, and CARMEL, 46, are cases in point. They have just returned to working in a local supermarket as cashiers after a 26 and 23-year absence from the work-force respectively. Far from being regarded as a liability they are highly valued members of staff.

CARMEL: "If someone said to me I would be out of work for 23 years I never would have believed them. But you get wrapped up in your children, they become your whole life. I was a hotel receptionist — the type of work I love. In a way this job is the same because I meet lots of people.

"It took me two whole years to work up the courage to apply for the job. I came up with lots of excuses. It was really a lack of confidence on my part. I would advise women who feel like that to go and do the 'women returning to the work place' course in FÁS to get their self-esteem back, and not to believe for a second your age will stand against you. It's an asset!"

MARINA: "I didn't lack confidence. I believed I would get a job again. I did go out to work as a childminder and housekeeper, but that was just an extension of what I was doing at home. It was the isolation that got to me — I wanted to be out meeting people again. And that's exactly what I am doing now.

"I feel I had my children too young, other women my age have 10 and 11 year olds. But the advantage was I discovered there was another side to life when I was still young. My youngest turned 18 three years ago. I had to find a way back into working life. I got my CV together and I applied for jobs for three years before this came up. The money isn't marvellous but it's mine and I love that feeling."

The European Foundation for the Improvement of Living and Working Conditions will publish findings later this year from its research project, 'Combatting Age Barriers in Job Recruitment and Training'" to which seven member countries contributed. Let's hope it will begin to redress the balance in favour of those who have worked hard for a long time — and deserve some credit.

EXERCISE
The reality spread-sheet

This exercise will take 15 minutes or so and will supply those daunted by the prospect of re-entering the work force with a few simple facts:

Take a piece of paper and a pen and write down the professions you are most interested in, or admire, or dream about, along the top of a page. Along the side write in the groups of people in your life. Now fill in the times, as a wife and mother and homemaker and community worker and unpaid farm labourer, you had to develop characteristics vital in those professions. The following example was done by Marina. She's never been idle for one second of her life:

	Accountant	Politician	Actress	Diplomat	Social worker
Family	Ran a house on a shoe string budget for years, kept it in the black		Pretended not to worry about kids. But sat up all night		
Friends					Provided help when needed. Listened when asked. Trained in drug awareness coaching skills
Community	Secretary of athletic club. Entrusted to handle funds and sign cheques			Held peace on committee meetings over the years — too many!	
Authority		Persuaded local authority to give grants and training needed in this area			
Schools				Involved with my kid's school from Day One. Attended all PTA's for 23 years	

And Marina is the sort who, when asked, doesn't feel she's done many exceptional things.

Facing the big 4-0

FIONA, 39 is reaching the milestone age:

"As I approach 40, I feel pretty happy with myself. I'm interested in growing as a person and in finding out more about myself, the universe, the whys and wherefores and what we're here for. The spiritual area of my life has become very important.

"I feel myself at a stage of re-evaluation. I'm fit and I look well for my age. I accept the changes that age is bringing — the flabby bits and loose bits. I still feel good about myself and am not paranoid about lines and ageing.

"I'm thinking in terms of: 'What do I want out of life? What changes do I need to or want to effect? Will I go back to college?

"Timing is important. I'm just about keeping my head above water at the moment and I'm wary about going back to college and having everything fall apart at the seams. I have to question myself as to whether this is genuine fear or an excuse. The current thinking is to put it off for a year and give myself another 12 months of reflection before I go for the commitment.

"When you get to your late 30s, early 40s you throw out a lot of crap. You're comfortable in your skin. It leaves you much more free, open and honest. It wasn't always like this. I found my teenage years very tough.

"I couldn't wait to grow up and be 20 and everything was wrong. I couldn't turn sideways in a bar because my nose was too big and I wouldn't play sport because my legs were so long and skinny! I had a terrible blushing problem, exacerbated by the fact there was a boys school right outside my house and I had to walk by hoards of them on a daily basis. I used to pray that my parents would move. The steam used to come out of my head.

"I would be very happy to have the body I had then with the confidence I have now. I don't think the combination would be allowed. It would be lethal! Men would have nowhere to hide!"

Being age-shy is not just about lacking assertion or feminist principles. You can have those and still be petrified by wrinkles spreading all over you like a crow playing havoc in a sandpit.

NOREEN, 53, is widely recognised among women's groups as a dynamic, pragmatic, get-things-done, intelligent female. They voted her Chairwoman of the National Women's Council. But even she has her weaknesses:

"This is so ridiculous, a real story about myself. When I was 50 my daughters were planning a party to celebrate and I was completely freaked at the idea, because up until then I had convinced myself and everybody else that I was two years younger. I had spent my whole life docking two years off my existence. On the one hand I was this highly sensible, very articulate woman and on the other hand I was harbouring this secret.

"I tried saying no to the party, hid behind excuses. But they were hell-bent on having it. So I came out on my 50th birthday. Most people couldn't believe it.

"I just thought that if people knew I was 50 they would see me in a totally different light. I think part of the reason for starting to lie was that my hair was going grey. Once I had verbalised the lie I had to stick to it, for 20 years, maybe 30... I feel so relieved now, because it became a big burden, it was like a big family secret... "

Noreen can now laugh at herself. But for many women age is no laughing matter.

SARAH, 25: "My mum and all her friends are disappearing off to have surgical nips and tucks, just to stop themselves from looking any older. I think it's pathetic now but maybe when I get to their stage I'll be doing exactly the same thing!"

But some women feel pressure from men to stay young, particularly due to factors like media coverage of the male menopause, which seems to involve the men running away with young nymphets and having six children, while the first brood and spouse starve in a garret. Doesn't do much for a woman's self-esteem to know this possibility lies ahead should his mid-life crisis spiral out of control.

Ageism isn't just the proviso of females doing battle with gravity.

MAEVE is a well-read, well-travelled, intellectual, affectionate, witty, discerning, attractive woman. She's just landed a role in a major new theatre production, which President Robinson will have seen at a gala evening by the time this book is on the shelves. Her self-esteem, individuality and love of life bowl you over. Especially when you take on board the fact she's 15.

Talking to her inspires pangs of envy when you recall your own stringy attempts to be sophisticated and mature at her age. She sees herself as having all a lot of advantages:

"My parents don't treat me like a child. I've always been treated like an adult. I have been asked what I thought and was always trusted. So I've always felt in control of my situation. This year I started going to pubs. My mother copped this instantly and said she would prefer if I didn't. So I don't. She said she prefers if I am honest about where I am going, because then she can make a judgement based on truth, rather than a lie. I respect this.

"If you're under the age of 18 in this country you don't count. You're still treated like a child. There's a real barrier there. You know you're a lot older than society gives you credit for. It's a pain in the ass when people don't listen to what you have to say or don't take it seriously because of this.

"I feel about seven years older than I am supposed to be! I've grown up a lot in the last three years, mainly because I have been lucky enough to travel a bit. Many of my friends are older and that has a lot to do with it too. I'm at a really tricky age where all the guys my age are still immature, but an 18 year old wouldn't look at me. I'm constantly attracted to older men and I feel like a freak sometimes.

"Landing this part in the play has been such an eye opener. For the first time outside my home I am being treated like an adult and given responsibility for myself. My friends are all in the late teens, early 20s and I feel like I have a lot in common with them. They certainly don't judge me by my age but by who I am.

"Nothing is legal at my age — nothing! I'll just have to wait until my age catches up with the rest of me. "

"When I am old I shall wear clothes that don't suit me, with a hat that doesn't go. I shall spend all my pension on brandy and summer gloves." — Jenny Joseph, Rose in the Afternoon

> *"Ageing is like almost everything else in life, to make a success of it — you've got to start young."* — Fred Astaire.

Looking back at your life

If you are uncertain about what you want to do with your life, and would like the benefit of having an old head on young shoulders, try this for size.

Imagine you are an old woman, looking back at her life. Imagine what this old woman, your old self, has done with her life. Work back through your life from decade to decade until you reach the age you are now. Put each decade on a separate sheet of paper.

Now arrange those sheets of paper in reverse order. You have a life plan starting from now and finishing when you are an old woman. Who needs a fortune teller when you've got you — and a measure of optimism!

Further reading

Directory of Services for Older People In Ireland
Age Action Ireland

What's Happening to My Body?
A Growing Up Guide for Parents and Daughters
by Lynda Madaras
Penguin

A Woman in Your Own Right
by Anne Dickson
Quartet Books

The Mirror Within
by Anne Dickson
Quartet Books

Our Bodies Ourselves
by Angela Phillips and Jill Rakusen
Penguin Books

Chapter Four

~~~~~~

SLAVE TO THE RHYTHM
Stress and its impact on your life

"Women think the world is going to stop if they don't keep it revolving.
But it continues to get on without us." — Brídín

WHEN WE LOOK BACK and observe the '90s from the next millennium, it will most likely be known as the decade where stress took centre stage. Dealing with its consequences has become a multi-million pound industry. It's now widely recognised as the the largest cause of absenteeism from work. It pervades every aspect of our lives. Even our sleep can be stressful, as we toss and turn deliberating over problems. An estimated 30% of the population suffer from insomnia.

Stress is basically defined as the demands made on your mind and body. If you have the capability to enjoy and meet those demands you are enjoying the positive benefits of stress. This is known as Eustress — think of it as a good personal assistant who sets the agenda for your day and helps you keep pace with it.

The problem arises when it gets a promotion to head of your department. It's then known as Distress and it is a megalomaniac with only one object: to turn you into a slave, a slave to its own rhythm. You find you cannot cope and your physical and mental resources become depleted, you feel overwhelmed and a victim of your own stress levels.

There are those who believe stress is a modern excuse for inertia. So, like depression, there is a stigma around admitting you're too stressed out to cope.

EDWINA DUNNE is Head Occupational Therapist at St James's Hospital, Dublin. She also lectures and runs workshops for community groups and businesses on stress. Although the general public may be only coming to terms with the concept in recent years, she argues that stress has been around since the dawn of time:

"It is a fight or flight reflex. It's part of our survival instinct. But, because it is such a basic response when we reach the running or fighting stage we're not using our higher thinking."

We're our own worst enemies. We are not in thinking mode therefore we start running, we start fighting, we start arguing. Basically, we're in trouble.

'Why am I always late?'

"Women are not just the fairer sex, they're the later sex." — Some Annoyed Man.

EDWINA has a pressurised job and a full family life. How does she manage to take it all in her stride?

"I have a helicopter, and I think everyone should have one too."

This is no Marie Antoinette brush off. It's a simple lesson in reality.

"I used to have a meeting in — say — Trinity at 11am, and I'd leave my desk here at James's at ten to eleven. I'd kill myself getting there... and it would still always take me half an hour to find a parking space and arrive. I'd be in absolute stress mode by the time I got to the meeting — and I'd be late anyway.
"This went on for a while, so I reasoned it out with myself. I came up with my Helicopter Concept. The only realistic way I was going to get to where I was going in ten or 15 minutes, was by helicopter. So I drew one and stuck it over my desk.
"Now, I do not take on 10 things-to-do an hour before I'm due somewhere. They have to wait. I just look at my helicopter and I know what the consequences are in staying. Elizabeth, my secretary, reminds me of my appointments by referring to my helicopter, which works.
"From a female point of view I suppose it's the Superwoman Syndrome that gives rise to high stress levels. Women are becoming aware of the traps involved in doing too much but I know many women who try to do everything. And, not only that, they expect to do everything really well.

I'm doing all I can
KATHLEEN, 30s, has learned to chop her own and family's high expectations of her down to size. She is no longer the magician and magician's assistant rolled into one:

"I get it at home — 'Mum, you're always late.'
"But then I'm the one who has to get the baby out. I'm the one who has to change the nappy. I'm the one who checks out everyones' needs. Has so-and-so gone to the toilet? Have I got my list? Have I got my money? Have I got my keys? Are the lights off? Are the doors locked?
"I have to also foresee the future. Where we are going, what do we require when we get there and do I have to cook dinner when I come back? Have I got it organised? Is the automatic oven on?
"By the time I slide into the car I can be knackered and not in the mood for going out. By the time I arrive, I'm dead. I skulk in the back seat. Then the kids and husband start:

'Why don't you ever sit in the front seat?' 'Why don't you ever volunteer to be on some of the committees at school or at the local clubs?'

"I don't volunteer because I can't do any more than I'm doing already. I have accepted that. To take on committee work and kill yourself completely is for women who like doing too much. I just say to my family that this is all I'm able to do. They've come to terms with it really. I'm being realistic and it makes life easier all round."

EDWINA praises this approach as accepting your limits and operating within them, an essential part of stress management:

"You can try to do everything, but I've come to the conclusion it doesn't really work. You have to learn limits. The ones who don't, well, maybe they give themselves unrealistic aims. Who is their role model? Perhaps their mother? Quite often in stressful situations a role model can be directly or indirectly responsible for the person feeling they can't cope.

"I think many daughters, quietly, resent their mothers. They feel that they have to compete with them in some way."

This is certainly true of **JOANNE**, 27:

"Whenever I felt ill or unable to cope at school my mother would say, 'That is your lot in life. Keep going.' I learned to go to school no matter how I felt. I felt guilty unless I got myself out of my sickbed and trudged into the classroom. I drove myself into the ground looking for my mother's appreciation and acceptance. I just kept working, working, working. I still do it. Even though the stress has such a negative impact on my life. I'm an everything-holic.

"I work hard at everything: relationships, friendships, socialising... even my hobbies are all hard work. The sad things is I know I can never achieve perfection. I can never work hard enough. I'm so used to the feeling of inadequacy I don't know how to live without it."

How do you recognise distress?

There are some experts who say there are many types of stress, but from a general standpoint stress is either good or bad for you.

EDWINA: "Distress means you're out of control. You feel like 'I can't think. I haven't got my own thoughts. I can't function properly. I've either got too many people pressures or too many time pressures.' When you start getting tired, you start going into Distress. Even if you have been feeling good, if you don't take rest, you become Distressed."

Since everyone is different the signs and symptoms for Distress vary. The only way you start recognising Distress, is to learn the signs and symptoms in relation to yourself.

"There are key questions:
    "What does my body feel like when I start feeling Distressed?
    "What happened to me to get me into this state?
    "You start teaching yourself: 'Now I'm beginning to feel this

tiredness. I begin to slow up. I can't bring myself up again. I'm tired. I'm not thinking straight.'

"You have to learn how to stop and take time out. Have a walk, have a stretch, have a yawn. Maybe do a relaxation technique. Then you can go back, feeling good again, for a period of time.

Sometimes you need a longer time than a few minutes relaxation to recover, but many of us feel that we are indispensible and don't allow ourselves to take the necessary time needed:

WINNIE, 54, has a working day that starts at dawn and ends at dusk, she and her husband run a farm:

"I was brought up on a farm. I think people have this notion that it's absolutely idyllic, like it is portrayed in the films. No way. We work all day and do accounts and orders in the evening. We hardly talk about anything else.

"Since I felt ill and developed heart trouble I have not taken any more chances with my stress levels. I can't say to cows 'milk yourself' but I can say to the husband and helpers 'I've too much to do to dish up a dinner at one o'clock'. They have to make do with soup and sandwiches. I gave Superwoman back the cape. It didn't look well on me!"

If you're stressed, you're often the last person to recognize that you are, that you need conscious, rational reasoning and thinking to do something about it.

ORLA, 30, went through a very stressful period five years ago, when her job got on top of her:

"I just went to the brink, and I felt the next step was a break-down. It was that close. The build up was gradual so I did not see myself changing at all. Then, towards the end, the whole thing escalated.

"I also had problems in my home life, so I couldn't go home and relax. I was given too much work to do, but for some unknown reason, I kept taking it all, I never said no. I think women in general don't — not like guys. I got so bad, that I didn't care about anything any more. I just felt that I couldn't cope. It got really intense, for a month or six weeks. My head was buzzing all the time. It wasn't a headache, it was just like I was a spring, coiled up. I wasn't sleeping well.

"I had lists of things to do every day in work, and I never got them all done. For a month, at least, when it was at its most acute, I kept thinking, 'there's no light at the end of the tunnel'.

"My employers were completely unaware that I was under any stress, which was partly my fault, but partly theirs as well. Their awareness level was zilch.

"The circumstances were a bit extreme so the state I was in was extreme. It got to the point, one week, where I just couldn't cope and I burst out crying a few times. That was the worst week. I started crying, for no reason — in the office.

"I rang my mother from the office one night, with the same thing — uncontrollable crying. I was working horrendous hours.

"The breakthrough came because I had planned a month's holiday and I couldn't get out of it. The night before I went I worked until 3 am on my computer and left lists of things for people. Then I packed in the middle of the night and got ready to leave at 6am for my holiday.

"For the first two weeks I was demented, and the two friends that I went with were driving me nuts. But it wasn't them, it was me, I was just trying to unwind and was extremely irritable.

"By the time I came back I was much better, much more relaxed and I knew what I had to do. I went to my Managing Director and told him I couldn't take any more, I had gone beyond the limit of endurance at that stage and I talked really frankly to him. My eyes were still glazed over from lack of sleep, even after a month's holiday. I told him I was overworked, exhausted, and I just spat all this out at him. I must have looked really wired to the moon, because he listened to me.

"He told me I was a valuable employee and to leave it to him, he would tell my two superiors to ease off, and he did, because my workload decreased significantly for the next three months. I built up to a normal workload again gradually.

"I still don't know what I was even doing it all for.

"But tackling the cause of the stress made me realise how good I was at what I do. So then I renegotiated my salary. I also got a new deal and a job description in writing.

"When you are stressed out beyond belief it is very difficult to think things through, you have to first deal with your anxiety. I would never have taken these steps if I had not had a month off to unwind.

"This gives you perspective and the perspective allows you to see just how valuable you really are. Women are very bad at setting limits for themselves, they want to accommodate all the time.

"If the sky fell down now, I would handle it. Because I would not see it all as my responsibility."

Orla found her way back to normality, but it could easily have gone the other way. How do you learn to be a good stress manager? Edwina feels maturity has a lot to do it.

"With maturity comes the confidence to say 'No,' or to say 'I don't understand what you mean. Explain it to me'."

Examination stress

AMANDA, 21, lost her appetite, couldn't sleep, became irritable, underweight and stopped exercising before her Leaving Certificate four years ago. Now she is a trainee veterinary nurse. Because she is working full-time and studying she has learned the necessity of proper routines and breaks while working up to exams.

"I just didn't cope coming up to Leaving Certificate. I did more worrying than studying. Because the exams are built up to be so important you have to cope with that pressure as well as a heavy workload. I lost a lot of weight. I was nervy and strung up.

"I dealt with it in that I got through it. I didn't contemplate topping myself or anything. But I know plenty of others who have. One person I know took a lot of pills because of the pressure on her at home. There is far too much emphasis put on the Leaving.

"After sitting up half the night, cramming and walking into exams half-dead the next morning I left school only to realise the results meant very little in the outside world.

"Now I am working full-time, attending lectures and sitting exams the pressure is even more intense. I realised I could not adopt a cramming approach so I have worked out a routine which helps. They are incredibly difficult exams, hardly anyone gets them first time. But if you really want to do something you stick at it. I don't let the stress get to me.

"I have trained as an athlete for most of my life and coming up to the Leaving Certificate I really let this go. Now I realise how important it is to maintain physical fitness because it keeps you alert and relaxed. No matter how much study I have to do, I work out.

"To young women sitting exams I would warn them that it is a very hard slog. Take breaks and try to explain to your parents that the breaks are as essential as the study.

"But most importantly — remember you and your health are more important than any exam. If you feel you cannot cope talk to someone immediately."

Edwina feels young women are under terrible pressure:

"The pressure of growing up, entering into the adult world, is very difficult for young women. The idea of it to me is just so exciting, but to many women it's intimidating and frightening.

"Because there are so many demands.

"We went to college and we had so much fun. Now I see my daughter thinking of college with apprehension. That concerns me.

"I think college is about growing up and having fun while you work hard. Like most things in life it's about balance. It's not about working all the time. When else in your life are you going to have this kind of space to grow up and explore new things? Try things out? That's what college is about. It's education in its broadest sense, not just about being educated in a profession or learning sphere.

"Points are all about numbers and places in college. They are not a measure of personal development, yet they are seen as such. I think it even inflates students' egos, in the sense that they got into a faculty that demanded high points; therefore they feel 'I am more intelligent than any of the rest of you'. But that's not the most important thing. The ability to get on with people is just as vital. There are people who do medicine who don't like people."

Something's got to give

Your emotions are good stress indicators. Orla mentioned her inexplicable crying bouts. Quite often tears are a sign to us of how much pressure we're under and how much we need to do something about it.

EDWINA: "Females are, in general, not frightened to cry, which is good — because it is not a sign of weakness, I see it as a sign of strength. You're confident enough to allow your emotions to happen. Hanging onto your emotions, not letting them out, is a lot worse. I have some people referred to me here suffering with panic attacks. Panic attacks can arise from inexpressed emotions, feelings have been suppressed to such an extent they become unmanageable.

"Basically, they can't breathe properly. The more they gasp for air the more frightened they become. In extreme cases, they will pass out. In less extreme cases they will feel terribly stressed and uncomfortable, until they're able to control yourself again.

"Panic attacks are not as uncommon as you might think, and can happen even to the most high-level thinker. We are all very vulnerable to them, if we don't control our stress.

"In one group a few years ago I had a young woman who was in a fire. They managed to rescue her, and everything was alright, but she began to have panic attacks about being locked in. She was off work for a long time but she worked through it because she was able to accept that stress existed and was something she needed to deal with.

"There was a University Professor, who had been through a serious illness and found it difficult to express his emotions around that. Even though, intellectually, he understood what was happening. I suggested that he might use relaxation techniques but he said: 'It's a lovely idea Edwina. Thank you very much. However I understand all of this.' Six months later he was back, saying 'I've had the most awful panic attack.' So he came into the group, where this young woman was participating. She had never been to college but she was able to teach him a lot about stress and expressing your emotions under stress. It was such fun. He had never met anyone like her in his life and enjoyed her thoroughly!"

Learning to de-stress

Stress management takes time. We have to accept it as a problem and then we have to learn how to deal with it. It may take a while before we feel any benefits.

EDWINA: "Techniques of recovery have to be part of a whole life plan. Relaxation for Living, the method I teach, takes time and involves the physical, physiological and social aspects of our lives.

"I teach people — first of all — to understand what stress feels like. Physically, what do I feel like when I'm stressed? What does my body feel like, when I'm stressed?

"Then we look at the psychological issues when we have got in touch with ourselves again. People then recognize what it is and also they look at the whole area of balancing their lives for release. In other words, 'How can I relax?'

"Some people want me to give them a magic formula. I don't possess one. With a lot of digestive problems such as heartburn, pains in the stomach, ulcers, indigestion, people come into hospital and have very complicated tests, they want a magic pill that will stop all these pains.

"It may very well be caused by stress but if they accept this they will have to do something about their lives, they will have to do something about themselves. In some cases they don't want to do that."

Edwina feels a lot of the fear is based on the feeling that to relax is to become lazy. Learning relaxation is not about becoming lazy. It's about balancing what you do. It's about becoming more efficient and more effective. It's about being in control.

'On reflection' — taking a step back from stress

FIONA, 39, has had to take a step back from her life, following a period where she felt unable to deal with the pressures on her:

"I've always tried to cope with stress on a preventative level. I play sport twice a week. I've had massage for 10 years. The more you tune into your body the better able you are to assess how you're getting on, which is why I was so surprised when things caught up on me.

"By the time I realised I was Distressed it was too late. I was too far gone to cope and had to stop completely. Instead of taking a few days bed-rest and then being back to normal, I recognised I had reached a point where I was physically and emotionally exhausted and no longer able to continue. My body caved in to the extent that every time I sat down on the couch I fell asleep. When I pulled up in the car park to play a game of tennis I fell asleep before I got out of my car. I was getting a very strong message from my body — 'I need rest and I need it badly.' I normally get up at 7.30am and go through a busy day before getting into bed at 11. But I need lots more sleep now. So I'm taking it. I've decided not to cook the Sunday roast or dinner every evening. I will not entertain people even though I love nothing better than to cook and have dinner parties.

"And I've expressed myself. I told family and friends 'I am not coping here, I'm under pressure, I'm not feeling well and need help.' Something I have never done before. It was very hard but the results were worth it. My husband would say 'Drop the potatoes, we're going out!' or 'Let's have a sandwich instead'.

"Go with your body, believe it. It's really the best barometer of how you are. My head can take me to all sorts of places which may not be realistic. The body is the best guide. If it's tired you're tired — a very simple message but a very hard one to get through to the old head. And if women think they are wimping out by taking such a course of action let me say this to them: think of the people having heart attacks at 40, ulcer diagnoses at 35.

"Set yourself different goals. You work hard to get things and to take care of your family. Realistically in a lot of cases you don't need the new car, the new garage, the holiday in the sun, the private schools to be happy. You need to live your life. Do you really get to enjoy the proceeds of what you're working for?

"I live with a man whose job is stressful beyond belief. I ask him — 'Is this worth it? I don't need any more than I already have. The children don't need it. So why do you keep working harder?' If you abuse your body the way he has abused his over the years you will not live to a ripe old age. And to live with that is stressful too. I love him. I don't want to see him leave us a second before his expiry date! The reality is we are expendable.

"I have to say I admire my husband for the way he takes care of us. He has a huge responsibility, sole breadwinners, male or female, aren't often acknowledged for bringing home a wage to support their families. It does suit me to be at home for the moment, but I can't deny I'm also here in the hope he won't have a heart attack if I look after the rest of our lives.

"I think what has happened to me has been a real wake-up call to the whole family."

Using the 'EU'-factor

If you use stress to your advantage this is known as Eustress. You're in the driving seat, you balance the scales, you set the limits. The whole function of stress is to save your life in a time of crisis and make you perform. It makes you do things. It makes you achieve. This biological response can help you run faster, think quicker, react better.

NIAMH, 29, is a television producer and self-confessed stress lover:

"I love it. I absolutely love it! There is nothing I like better than being in a studio and fighting against the clock on a live TV programme. I am made for deadlines. They bring out the best in me. It does not affect my appetite or sleep, although sometimes I am so busy I forget to eat. People complain about their high pressured jobs all the time but the truth is I could not live without mine. I get the biggest buzz from it.

"In college I was always the one who had nothing done until a day before deadline. So I have found the perfect job for me. There are drawbacks but none that would make me reconsider my options. I know it's unhealthy not to see daylight from one end of the day to the other, so I try to make myself go out for walks. I'm actually sure people are concerned because I am so happy. Very strange."

Not my problem

A huge factor in stress avoidance is not allowing people to give you their problems. EDWINA calls this the 'Monkey on the Shoulder' syndrome.

"There is a whole saga about the monkey on the shoulder. Someone comes to my door, and they have a problem. They say 'Can I talk to you about my problem?'

"But what they're really saying to me is: 'Can I give you my problem?'

"So the monkey that was on their shoulder, hops over to my shoulder. I take their problem and they go away. They feel great, but I have another monkey to join the colony on my shoulders.

"Now, when you see this coming it's up to you to say: 'Okay, you have a problem. Let's talk about it. What can **you** do to solve it'."

Coping with 'No way out'

There are some situations thrust upon us, such as poverty and unemployment, which can be stressful no matter what we do. In the book 'Nervous Breakdown' based on the RTE radio series, psychologist Edward Hogan points out in his essay on stress:

"...Studies consistently indicate lower levels of psychological ill health among the long-term unemployed when compared with the employed population."

Living with unemployment is stressful. Living with the poverty imposed by unemployment is stressful. **ESME**, 42, is a woman who lives with both:

"We took a decision to bring up my granddaughter so my daughter could have a life, go to school and that. Now she has a job, I take care of the child.

"We have struggled for years. My husband is what they call long-term unemployed. He does not even bother looking for work now. He is sick of the knock backs. This causes terrible upsets in the house. I get fed up with him under my feet. We lost the knack of love years ago.

"My life is a constant penny pinch. My brother helps me out if we get into difficulties but I still have my pride. Although we have not often faced the prospect of no food on the table, we have times when we are hungry and there is no cheque until tomorrow.

"The local resource centre gave me free financial advice, but I don't have any finances! They did a budget with me and it only showed me exactly what I thought. If I died tomorrow I would not have a penny.

"When I went on a stress-management course I learned ways of releasing the tension caused by the pressure I am under. I now do things that don't cost anything. I go for walks, visit friends.... I enjoy treating myself to a hot shower with a drop of oil to rub into my skin. Sometimes I get the family together, it's harder now they're all in their teens — we turn the telly off and talk about things.

"When I started to do it they thought I was mad. But now they listen a bit. When I feel like the burden is too big I lock myself in the bedroom and turn on the radio. I look at the sky and watch the clouds and imagine I am on one and going somewhere. I cry sometimes. Then I go back outside and face the music."

EDWINA, like most of us, is filled with sympathy for Esme's situation.

"It's a real trap, a poverty trap. You ask yourself: 'Where am I going?' Many times I have heard women say: 'My life's awful, I have nothing.' Where's their self-esteem?"

But occasionally one woman finds a way through and gives inspiration to others:

EDWINA: 'I would urge women in the unemployment/poverty trap to contact community groups, or GPs. Find someone who can help and talk to them. Women who have done this — in my experience — have proved inspirational for other women, sharing the same predicaments."

Stress and your GP
For women who fear their GP might prove unsympathetic, **RACHEL**, 32, has this advice:

"I would recommend that any woman feeling stressed out to get in touch with her GP. They're now so aware of the long and short term effects of stress they can really help you come to terms with your workload. Once, when I was really worked up and couldn't function properly, I went to my doctor. She examined me, talked to me and told me I needed to take three weeks off work. She listened to me when I talked about the causes of the stress, and suggested I start dealing with them, once I had the chance to recover. Even if employers don't accept the effect of stress, and many don't, doctors do if they're anyway understanding."

EXERCISES

1. AM I STRESSED OUT?

If you answer 'yes' to one or more of these questions the chances are your stress levels are high and you need to look at ways of bringing them back to normal again. In their excellent handbook *Understanding Stress*, available from most chemists, Prof Greg Wilkinson and Dr Tony Smith pinpoint some mental and physical symptoms to watch out for:

MENTAL SIGNALS

Do you feel under pressure?
Do you feel tense and unable to relax?
Do you feel mentally drained?
Are you constantly frightened?
Are you aware of being more irritable or moaning more than usual?
Do you sense conflict within yourself?
Is there a feeling of frustration or aggression there?
Are you sometimes restless, unable to concentrate or finish tasks quickly?
Are you crying more?
Is your manner more suspicious and pessimistic?
Do you feel unable to make decisions?
Are you aware of an impulse to run and hide?
Do you have an imminent fear of fainting or collapse?
Do you worry about failure?
Do you worry about making a show of yourself in public?
Do you feel unable to enjoy life?

PHYSICAL SIGNALS

Has your breathing speeded up?
Has your appetite changed?
Do you feel over-alert?
Have you problems getting to sleep?
Are you jumpy?
Do you get headaches, chest twinges, eye twitches
Do you have increased indigestion, frequent need to pass urine?
Do you have a dry throat/mouth?
Are you constipated or do you have diarrhoea?
Do you feel tired or weak a lot?
Are there butterflies in your stomach?
Are you sweating a lot?

2. ACHIEVEMENT DIARY

Often when you feel low and demoralised it can be hard to drag yourself back up again. Invest in a little pocket diary. A line per day is all you need. Write in it all the things you have achieved in your day. From getting up, to getting exercise, to making a phone call you intended to make for ages. Just by appreciating the smallest things you do well, you will gain the confidence to look at the bigger issues.

3. BODY OBSERVATION AND BREATHING

This is an exercise, recommended by the Relaxation for Living organisation. It focuses you on your breathing and allows you in turn to focus on yourself.

Sit or lie in a well-supported and comfortable position. Wear clothes that are loose. Relax your tummy. Place one hand on your navel and one on your upper chest. Have your elbow supported if possible.

— *Let your breath go*
— *Breathe in very gently, feeling your abdomen rise slightly under your lower hand*
— *Breathe out again, equally gently, taking a fraction longer than you did breathing in. Feel your abdomen drop back again.*
— *Pause for a moment*
— *REPEAT*

Unless you are smothering with a cold, breathe in and out through your nose. Try to have as little movement as possible underneath the hand resting on the upper chest. The reason for you trying to exhale for longer is because breathing in involves muscle contraction and the heart and metabolism speed up slightly, breathing out involves relaxation and the heart and metabolism slow down.

Practise this for two or three minutes, several times a day. Gradually you will be able to do it without the hands and standing up.

Further reading

Understanding Stress
A BMA handbook by Prof Greg Wilkinson
Available in Chemists
Stress and Relaxation:Self-Help Techniques for Everyone by Jane Madders
Positive Health Guides
Macdonald, Optima
Stresswise
Lookes and Gregson
Hodden

■ *Consult the directory for information on organisations.*

Chapter Five

~~~~~

LEARNING TO BE SINGLE FIRST

I**T'S EASY TO FORGET** the word 'relationship' belongs to much more than marriage or partnership. It belongs to the person you share the deepest love with and to the stranger you share secrets with on a train and never see again. It belongs to everyone we come into contact with in our lives.

The only real certainty in relationships is they begin and end with yourself. Sharing your life with another human being is most fulfilling when you know who you are, and they know it too.

This chapter invites women to read and share their love and experience of being lovers, daughters, sisters, mothers, friends — and themselves. The experiences are not models of perfection, but they offer insight into the joys and pain they have known, with and through others.

To look at relationships from a female perspective we need to look at the links established from the moment we are born, with the outside world. Family Therapist **OWEN CONNOLLY** says:

> "A daughter will look to her mother in terms of learning the tools for living and how to be a woman. It's important for a mother to have pride in herself as a woman and to have sense of self-worth and esteem in order to give these gifts to her children."

The message is clear. You need to feel good about yourself in order to have good relationships.

Problems, problems

No relationship is without them, but where do you turn to solve the issues you can't work out together? Owen Connolly has been married to **CLAIRE** for 28 years. They travel the world giving conferences and counselling on relationships as counsellors trained in the Intimacy Centre of Therapy.

Their experience runs deeper than professional training. They were in trouble once themselves. Ironically it is Claire who persuaded Owen, now working full-time as a therapist, that they needed outside help:

OWEN: "We've had times when we felt we didn't want to be in the relationship. Times when we felt if the situation arose we would leg it. That's speaking for both of us."
CLAIRE: "I was keen to go to counselling. Owen didn't want to know about it. He spent a lot of time away, I spent a lot of time alone. My experience as a woman was you lose your identity, who you are as a person. First of all marriage is romantic and wonderful, then children come on the scene, the focus goes on to them, you find you are spreading yourself out and there isn't enough to go around. You wake up one day and you realise you haven't given any time to yourself."
OWEN: "And it's exactly the same for men. Where things went wrong for me was where they go wrong for a lot of people who enter a relationship not fully aware of what it involves. Children can be an interruption. At first I was euphoric about becoming a father but suddenly accountable, something I was not used to. Also the baby became very important to Claire and I was out of the picture."
CLAIRE: "As a couple, we came in between two generations. We married at the tail-end of the generation where you didn't work after marriage. So I gave up work and the child came soon after the marriage. Contraception wasn't available in the late '60s. Then the sands shifted and I found myself viewing a whole new generation of women who remained at work after marriage. I didn't know where I fitted in. And Owen couldn't help because he wasn't very communicative at the time.
OWEN: "Up to the age of 35 I was closed off emotionally, it would have been said of me that I would not even cry at my own mother's funeral if she died. There are a lot of women living in this country who have partners like that. How my wife was supposed to communicate with me was anyone's guess."
CLAIRE: "But we did learn to communicate. He was persuaded to seek help in time and out of sorting our own problems came the vocation to counsel others. We devote a lot of time to that now. We've been through the mill ourselves so we know how it feels for others to go through it."

So what are the main issues facing today's couples? Lack of communication and emotional expression would be top of the list.

CLAIRE: "We find a lot of couples our age are splitting up now after 25 years of marriage, because they have stayed together for the sake of the children and now the children have left there is nothing else, between them.'

Claire and Owen cannot stress enough the importance of continuing to invest in each other once you have children.

CLAIRE: "Your children will leave one day, and you will only have each other. Do not deprive one another.
"When you are emotionally deprived you attract emotionally deprived relationships. If our emotional needs are not met they just close down. This often happens today when our society pays little or no attention to our emotions.
"People are starving for comfort, affection and contact. That is the reason we are saying things like: 'S/he doesn't understand me'. People cannot communicate because they aren't relating at an emotional level."

CAOIMHE, 24: "I haven't had a relationship because I have a real lack of self-esteem.

This has made it difficult for me to relate to others and for them to relate to me. I would love to meet someone with whom I could be honest about my own feelings."

SAOIRSE, 28, has been married to **TONY**, 38, for five years. They decided to seek counselling in the second year of their marriage:

"I loved Tony and was very happy with him from the moment I met him. But I walked into marriage without realising just what it meant. A few weeks before the wedding I had a fling. I had never been unfaithful — the thought had never entered my mind. But getting married seemed such an enormous step and I got frightened at the prospect of never kissing, never making love to or dating another man.

"I told Tony, because we had always agreed to tell each other if there were problems. He was hurt and very angry but we talked it through and put it down to having pre-wedding jitters.

"I settled down after the wedding, but a year later I started to feel trapped and restless again. I think the age gap had something to do with it. He had done all his running around and growing up and I had a ring on my finger trying to do the same. I am ashamed to say I really began to hate him.

"My friends were all single and going out on the town, on holidays, swapping stories about chatting up men and new boyfriends. I felt so left out. I ended up getting drunk and pursuing men on more nights than I care to remember. But each time I would be contrite.

"Then it happened, someone else came along. A man who refused to give up until I agreed to meet him. He wrote to me, he sent me flowers at work. Tony was totally unaware and I was actually happier at home because I was getting romanced again instead of just being the wife.

"I had an affair. For me it was of the heart and for this other person it was of the penis.. This time I realised I could not go back... It had gone too far.

"Tony and I agreed I should move out. At this time he looked like death warmed up because he was as much in love with me as ever. I was still very uncertain.

"One day, months later, I took one look at him and realised I would find very few men to beat him in the consideration stakes. I asked him how he felt about us. He said 'I love you and I want us to be together, but I would rather go through this pain now than live with a woman who does not love me.'

"We talked and agreed to give it another shot. But before I moved home we went for counselling to sort out our problems.

"The counsellor did not judge either of us. She helped Tony realise my sense of insecurity and the fact I still had a lot of maturing to do. I came to realise a lot of my behaviour was to do with other needs.

"We are together again. I hope we stay together. It has not been perfect. I still feel like I have missed out on my youth a bit but then I have a very deep and fulfilling love with my husband and I see a lot of my single friends suffering with men who won't commit.

"We have talked about children but we are taking it easy — we're never rushing into anything ever again!'"

Love and marriage?

Many couples are opting for a long term-relationship without state or church endorsement. However you decide to express your love you will have the same emotional decisions to make: commitment, communication, compromise and breathing space all have to be considered.

LORRAINE, 26, has been living with **MICHAEL** for six years:

"Every time my mother sees us she drops hints about rings on fingers. I think I'll grow bells on my toes before that happens. I'm very happy with Michael and I want to be with him. That's enough for us at the moment. If children entered the equation I might feel differently but I think we have enough going for us without making it strictly legal.

"What I love about living with Michael is we are both here because we want to be here. I think we have a fairly equal relationship."

Disposable love

BETTY, 33: "I had one, one-night stand that lasted for a year."
MARIE, 25: "I was in the relationship for a year, he was in it for two months."
JANET, 37: "I waited 12 years for him to grow up and when he did he wanted someone else."

We live in a commitment-shy culture and one-night stands, plus condom if you're not crazy, are part of it. If you're lucky they spin out into a few dates but many men run a mile when they hear you suggesting a weekend away next month, never mind talking about wedding bells.

Who fares better out of the current relationship climate — men or women? CLAIRE and OWEN have considered this question long and hard — here are their thoughts.

CLAIRE: " Men definitely fare better. I challenge a lot of young guys who say 'not bad for a woman'. If the younger generation are still so sexist what hope is there for the future?"
OWEN: "If a man's nose was to glow every time he had an erection he would soon understand that he actually can take charge of his penis and therefore his sexuality. No one teaches men that they have authority and control over it. They have this idea that their sexuality has a mind of its own and they convey that message to women. This is 1996!'"

Women have arrived at a place where they have more choices to make, which may make things more difficult relationship-wise. At least your mother knew it was marry your father or else marry another man. Either way partnerships were for life and, for the most part, formalised in front of a priest.

Now that we have no set relationship patterns we enjoy more freedom. But it allows us to be even more commitment-shy, and can create emotional confusion.

CLAIRE: "Young girls I meet want all the things I did as a young woman. But they seem to have a fear of standing their ground and saying 'I want to get to know you before we have sex. They don't have the security of knowing relationships will progress to the engagement stage and the engagement will turn into a marriage.

OWEN: "I believe women are hurting more than men in today's relationships. As a family therapist I see women, after 20 or 30 years of marriage, who are devastated by their husband not wanting them anymore.

"And equally painful is to see a young woman who becomes attracted to a man who does not want the same things. Where she wants a relationship, the 'settling down' and 'having a family' instinct is not so strong with men

"The sad thing is to see young women starving for a relationship but unable to enter into one due to fear, fear of being abused, emotionally, physically, sexually. You're dealing with a lot of isolation here in 1996 on the male and female side of things."

When you meet someone you do have rights. Most importantly the right to know where you stand. Many of the women I talked to who were commitment-shy were so because they had been hurt and did not want to be so again.

ORLA, 29: "You can really lose your independence in a relationship."

CLARE, 40: "My main reservation in entering a relationship would be because the last one left me badly hurt."

VIOLET, 29: "I constantly feel dissatisfied in relationships and want something other than what I have. Perhaps I have a fear of settling down."

Trust and respect were top of the list of relationship needs with the women surveyed. But to find trust and respect you have to be prepared to risk involvement. Maybe we need to find a common ground between marrying because it's the recognised path, as our mothers did, and allowing someone to come close enough to find mutual acceptance and a place to begin a deep, meaningful relationship.

Falling in love again...

GRAINNE, 40, might be doing just that, following the breakup of a painful and ultimately violent, marriage:

"It is three years since I left my husband. I had two crushes on people since then that shouldn't have really happened. I think it was because I was feeling insecure and I needed someone to back me up. My husband was being really threatening and determined to follow me wherever I went.

"I have never really felt lonely as a separated woman in the sense that I had loads of friends and I could fill my days with work but at night I felt alone. There is a real shortage of available men at my age. A friend suggested I put an ad in the paper. I got a group of friends together with a few bottles of wine and wrote out the advert. I got about 30 replies and have met a few. One of them is very nice and I am now seeing him.

"What scares me most about getting involved with someone now? That I will hurt somebody. My need for having my own self esteem boosted is greater than my ability to judge whether somebody is good for me or not. I feel a bit apprehensive about this person I have met for that reason. He has fallen for me. It has been very passionate.

"One of the things about meeting people through the small ads is that it is not like meeting at a party, where you indulge in small talk and wouldn't launch in to talking about marriage or your break-up, or what your relationship with your 'ex' is like. You put your cards on the table immediately and say what it is you want from the beginning.

"Recently I wrote down all the things I wanted from my life, everything I was grateful for, i.e. family, friends and even myself. If you have your goals clearly in mind, it gives you a focus. It was like putting the ad in the paper, you put down what you are looking for. Although you do have to treat most of the dates as entertainment value, you wouldn't want to go out thinking you are going to meet the man of your dreams.

"Advice to women who are starting out again? Take things slowly. Find 'you' first. I think I am still getting to know myself. I know I am a parent, that is me, but I am still not sure of the relationship side."

Rows and the broken fruit bowl

SARAH, 27: "We don't go a week without rowing. The best one was when I took the glass fruit bowl and smashed it on the floor. He shut up then. I like to think of them as passionate arguments."
CLAIRE has this to say about rows: "Rows are an essential part of any relationship in order to deal with the conflicts that must arise. The trick is to realise their reason for occurring and to resolve them to your mutual satisfaction. No matter how much you love your man you have to able to agree or disagree. It's very important because our opinions change from time to time on different issues."

Learning to be single first

Learning to be single before you get into a relationship is also an essential part of love. If we don't know and love ourselves how can we expect someone else to?

MARIA, 49, has been married to JOHNNY, for 24 years:

"I felt I had given everything to him and the children. When I turned 40 I felt more and more strongly that I needed to give something to myself. I looked for ways in which to do that and developed my own interests outside of the family home. It took my family a while to adjust to the fact that I was not there in the way I always had been. I still loved and cared for them, but I did not have dinner on the table every night if I had a class or a social event to go to. I think they appreciate me more because of it."

MARY, 30s: "Recently I learned to swim. And recently my husband learned to cook while I was out at swimming lessons. He's turned into a good cook and I've turned into a reasonable swimmer. I don't think it's my duty to bring up the children anymore — I think it's a joint responsibility. I let him have a say and he does his share of the parenting. It makes for a better relationship I feel."

ELAINE 30: "I have taught my husband about respecting women. He is a big, gentle man and I love him but, like a lot of Irish men, he was conditioned to believe my place was in the home. My place is in the world, like his."

JACKIE, 34: "The year was 1994. I was 32 and having spent 14 years nurturing my two children and being mother, lover and friend to my husband I decided to take a little time out for myself.

"I had been wrapped in this warm, loving cocoon for so long it was a daunting task to even consider what I wanted to do. I eventually decided on a FAS course, and to return to school as a mature student. It beat having my mind saturated with daytime soaps.

"I studied English and found I it rewarding and took to business skills like a duck to water. All those years organising everyone else paid off, I was a well-organised woman! It was a turning point in my life. When I collected my City and Guilds and Leaving Certificate results it was a very proud moment for me. I've now found part-time work in a terrific environment.

"There is life after buggies, bottles, bags and housework. The constant frustration is gone. All you need to do is get off your rear end and make it happen. There are plenty of schemes to help women like us get an education and a job and a restore our confidence in ourselves.

"I wasn't a bad mother or wife — I am a better one now. I also learned to drive in '94, and if I could do that anyone can."

FIONA LEAHY is a marriage counsellor with ACCORD who has advised many women like Jackie, who mightn't necessarily have relationship problems but are looking for themselves:

"A lot of women who come in the ACCORD centre are looking for something, not necessarily relationship counselling. They've lost their personal identity. They don't need to work on other people's involvement with them, they have to work on their involvement with themselves. Isolation is very often the hardest part of the problem. To be in a room with other women experiencing the same thing is such a relief. You very quickly get rid of the notion that everyone else is managing fine."

Being alone

ACCORD runs personal development courses for women to help them get in touch with themselves and hopefully, from that beginning their relationships. For some of us being alone can be a terrifying prospect, so we rush headlong from relationship to relationship.

Owen and Claire find this terror of being alone in many of the couples and individuals they counsel. The fear can strangle a relationship because neither partner can get breathing space:

CLAIRE: "You have to teach people to be separate before they can be brought back together. When their relationship is on the rocks, they need to look at each other as individuals. You may find that, perhaps, they had several other relationships they have never dealt with before they started a relationship with each other. So, you get the people to look at themselves and detach from the relationship until such time as they see it and themselves properly.

"I think that we are creating a lot of people who are very alone. They might have friends, but they are alone, they are frightened of being away from the headset or the video because their aloneness scares them."

NOREEN , 53: "Women invest far more emotional energy in relationships than men do, and I think that is a big mistake. My mother used to say things to me which I never understood, but now do, like: 'To man love is a thing itself to woman it's her whole life.'

"I think it's great to see young women, and now a lot of older women, who have a life outside relationships, staying in touch with their girlfriends, keeping interests and activities in their lives, and consciously so. We have more personal power.

"In my first marriage I lost that power. What happened to me very quickly was that all my friends were my husband's friends.

"Some people tend to just blame the man when that happens, but you do it to yourself. You know that business of 'We are now married so we are now one'. I think that is a trap for some women and I am sure for some men as well. Your oneness is with yourself."

SHARON, 30, is so happy with her own company she does not need a man unless he is right for her:

"People really think I am either a lesbian who has not come out to herself or I am having an affair. I think you should be happy with yourself before you start foisting yourself on other people. Women in particular feel that they have to gain their identity from somebody else. Unless they are part of a twosome they are not quite fulfilled

"I am a pretty well-rounded person , a relationship would be a welcome addition but I don't want just anyone. I want the right one.

"I am the odd one out in a society of couples. People are afraid of a single person. If I go to a dinner party I am put beside a single man who I have nothing in common with.

"There is serious social pressure to get hitched or at least get someone. I have never got to the stage that I wanted to give up everything for one man. I still have plenty of companionship in my life. I love to have an intimate dinner party with about four or five friends.

"I have no problem going out on my own, except maybe for a meal. I have often met people when I am out on my own and they will ask 'Who are you with?' When you tell them you're on your own they look at you as though you are really sad."

Alone, but not lonely

MOIRA, has come out of a marriage breakup that left her financially challenged and emotionally restored:

"Do you know what I would say to women? Talk to yourself, listen to yourself, that is what I do when I am sitting on my own. Feel the pain, don't be afraid of the memories. Even with a marriage breakdown don't be afraid of the memories, they are part of your past, part of your life, they are something that happened to you and they can't all be bad

"It took a hospital bed to persuade me it was over. They did tests on me and could find nothing wrong — yet I could not keep any food down. In the ward next to me were four women. All of them were addicted to Valium or Librium. They were all women in their mid-forties. They all had money, none of them was deprived. They really frightened me because they had the golf club membership, the two cars, the holidays twice-a-year, the big house, the private schools for their kids, clothes — everything, but they were all screwed up.

"I could see myself in that situation.

"What I saw in there gave me the courage to take the steps. I had known for a long time what I had to do but I was just so terrified. But it just got to the stage where I was more afraid of staying than of leaving. To stay with the money and the status I would have had to put up with circumstances which were not for me. Let me tell you I tried to make it work, for the sake of my family. But I couldn't.

"I also made the decision to stay at home and look after my children. To do the job of rearing them properly. I knew it would not happen if I, as a single parent, went out to work and came home with no energy to give them in the evening.

"That decision had financial repercussions. I lost the plush lifestyle. But I opted not to work full-time because I already had a successful career, that of raising children. I'm going for the pension!"

Communication and compromise

FIONA LEAHY, apart from being a marriage guidance counsellor, is also happily married with two sons:

"If you're happy in your relationship it certainly colours the rest of your life. In my experience where things go wrong is where communication has broken down.

"The corner stone of a good partnership is communication. If two people can talk about what's going on then they are in business. Especially when they can see each other's point of view. You can uncover for one another what exactly is going on and reach some realisation. There is nothing more satisfying than seeing a couple communicate after a bad patch. It's heartening.

"Another thing is learning to compromise. An old chestnut, but a true one. You cannot change a person to the extent they become exactly like you.

"And if you're going to tackle him and ask him to live up to your standards you have to have the confidence to chalk them up consistently. That requires courage because you will meet with resistance. And I can stick myself in this bracket."

MARY and **LOUISE** have had some difficulty in their relationship establishing exactly whose turn it is to do the laundry:

MARY: "Just because we're both women does not mean our house is spick and span. We both hate housework. But I am tidier than Louise, she would sleep in the same sheets for weeks if I could stomach it.

"I have come to realise I have a lower tolerance for mess. So as long as we are together I will end up doing most of it. But it doesn't stop me raising the roof occasionally.

LOUISE: "Actually I would dispute her argument! She is allergic to the hoover. Completely."

When you first meet someone it takes a while to get to know them and understand where they are coming from.

AMY and SHANE had to learn to commmunicate with each other when they first met. She didn't fancy him at first, he had never been out with someone who used a wheelchair:

AMY: "I was not impressed by him at all initially, he sort of grew on me. I had my eye on someone else at the time.

"He openly admits that before he knew me he would cross the road if he saw somebody in a wheelchair, for fear of saying the wrong thing to them or staring. He was very uncomfortable. It is not that able-bodied people deliberately set out to avoid those who have disabilities, it is just that they are embarrassed in case they cannot understand them, or are not able to help.

"Some of his relatives were not happy about our relationship but I reached a stage where I had to put it out of my head. If you are not given the opportunity to present yourself as an equal then there is no point in trying to get on with people.

"I think the main problem people with disabilities have in relationships is communication — meeting people. Up to now if you had a serious disability you would have had difficulty in socialising — due to lack of access. But that is changing all the time.

"I don't believe I ever saw myself as any different to any other woman, or thought in those terms. I had no reason to, I had lots of people that I would have been attracted to and vice-versa."

Loving women

JODIE, 29, and **CATHERINE**, 26 are truly, madly, deeply in love with each other.

JODIE: "The thing that women have in common with men is that they are human beings. Women are meant to be more understanding, but when it comes to it, a woman will sleep with someone, and throw them over just like a man will do.

"I was in a four-year relationship with someone and found out later she had been unfaithful. I am a very loyal person, and I felt betrayed. Then Catherine came into my life. I am so happy. I always knew that I liked her, I always got on well with her.

"There was a really short time span between the two relationships. I was afraid of hurting, but she said 'I care enough about you to see if that happens, and to ride the storm'.

"What I like about my relationship with Catherine is that I am now much more in touch with my straight friends than in my last relationship, I ostracised myself then, quite a lot and just moved around in Gay circles. Now we meet straight people do straight things. We will be ourselves, hold hands, put our arms around each other, give each other a kiss.

"We are like star-struck lovers. It is not always easy, you have to be careful in some places, you don't know who is watching, and might follow us some night and attack us. You cannot perceive what some people will do. I am very content in this relationship, very comfortable. I can see us buying a house together.

"I am my own person, I know our relationship is equal. I know lesbians where you can see who is taking the lead role and you can see those that are real wifey, wifey. Neither of us want children.

"We don't live together, but we practically do, we spend more time together than apart.

"The sticky bit is my family. My parents are both pensioners and though they are quite liberal for their age I am not going to rock the boat by telling them who I am in love with."

CATHERINE: "I get absolutely everything out of my relationship with Jodie.

"I've known her a long time but it took me a while to get to know what my own feelings were, so I didn't really think about Jodie in that way, not until a few years later. Until I knew how I felt about myself. I did have brief things with other women, but nothing like this.

"I told my brother and he seemed sound about it. My mum is very liberal minded but I don't know. I am hoping she will guess.

"I couldn't just put my finger on it, but I get something more with her than I did with men. I have gone out with a few, but I knew it wasn't what I wanted. It's partly emotional, partly physical, partly spiritual. To commit to her on a more public basis is not really feasible here at the minute. We know how we feel. I love everything about her, she is just brilliant."

Parenting

"Your children are not your children.
They are the sons and daughters of life's longing for itself...
You may give them your love but not your thoughts,
For they have their own thoughts."

– KAHLIL GIBRAN, "THE PROPHET"

MAGDELEN, 50s: "Mothers can rejoice when they see their daughters fully grown. They can see the input they have had into their daughters. My own came to me and said: 'Mum, it's wonderful that I have never once felt you were jealous of me. I always felt you were behind me. Now that I have moved out on my own I can see you as a person in your own right. And do you know, if you hadn't given me such confidence I might have felt jealous of you?' I felt my tears come when she said that.

"To hear something so positive about something so important. To know that you have done something right. I tell the young women I talk to to tell their mothers, only if they feel it of course, to tell their mothers they are good people who have done a good job. It's like the most important task of your life has been fulfilled."

OWEN: "As a parent you shouldn't have expectations for your children, some parents want their child to live out their own fantasy. I think that is very destructive. Children are very obliging, they want to please, they want to fix, they want to put right and they will walk away from their own instincts to fit in with you."

CLARE, 32: is a mother of two toddlers, here she shares her experience of being a daughter and a mother:

"I had a very happy and secure home but from the time I was four a full-time house-keeper came in and ran the whole show. My mother didn't want to know. She was not into the minutiae of constant childcare. My whole role model was a mother who was in high-heels, in the suit out doing her job. That's what I was conditioned towards becoming — well-heeled and professional.

"But from the time I had the kids I felt this pull to spend more time with them. I have a lot more patience than my mother. I enjoy the company of my kids even though it is very wearing. I am not that skilled at it because I was not brought up learning the skills.

"Little girls are brought up to be good girls. I do it all the time to my daughter and I am not supposed to. We have been brought up to be the carers who do the little things that make everybody happy. That is a female thing.

"My son gets away with murder. You fall right back into the same trap once you become a mother. You have kept up being the good girl and so you tend to expect your daughter to too."

ANNA, 42, has a 17-year-old son, **JONATHAN**, who is hooked on heroin. Their relationship is what has kept him wishing to live:

"If I couldn't sit here and talk to you about my son about being a drug addict I'd sit here and cry about it. I made a choice to put him out of the house. It was the hardest thing I ever had to do, but through counselling, I realised I had to let him go until he fell hard enough. He has missed his adolescence so he is still a child. A few weeks ago he took money from his sister out of her jeans and phoned me in work sobbing his eyes out. He knew he had done wrong but he couldn't help himself.

"I think the hardest thing any mother would have to do is to say to her 17-year-old son is: 'Get out and just don't come back until you want to stop'. I said to him, 'Jonathan I love you, you are my son and I love you from head to toe but you are a junkie. But I will never stop loving you or fighting for you.

"We are great pals, he kisses me and hugs me. I never stopped loving him, I just hated what he was doing to himself. The day I threw him out I stopped fighting him and started to fight the drugs. That was the day things turned around. I hope he will survive. He tells me he wants to kick it because he loves me so much he can't bear to go on hurting me."

Empty nest syndrome

When you have invested a lifetime in your children — how do you cope when they make their own lives and leave home? **MOIRA**, 46, is one woman coming to terms with this:

MOIRA, 46: "Most weekends now the children are gone. I was here on Saturday night on my own. Something I will have to do is discipline myself. It's very hard when you've been doing this job for years, 25 of them to be exact, and all of a sudden you don't have that job to do anymore.

"But I would say this. If they don't need you in the same way it is a very good sign. You have done a good job if they are confident enough to leave you. Just allow yourself time to adjust to that.

"Now I have freedom. The phone goes and someone asks me out on the spur of the moment. I can go!

"Set plans for yourself, goals you forgot about when the first baby came along all those years ago. I want to do drama, I'd like to join the Shakespeare Society, I want to paint, I want to cook more exciting food and entertain, I would like to travel more."

Female friendship

Female friendship is what we value above any other relationship outside our families. In many ways it is just as important to us. Who would be without it? Not any of the women I spoke to.

JENNIFER, 27: "I have many friends and I feel I need every one of them. Male company is not enough."

JULIE, 29: "My best friend is beautiful, honest and warm."

SARAH, 20: "Claire is brilliant, always takes my side."

MAGS, 26: "I learn so much from them."

ANNETTE, 32: "I value female friendship. I find it stimulating, infuriating, great."

GWEN, 24: "My best friend and I understand each other totally."

MADELEINE, 29: "Friendship is crucial to all human beings. It civilises us. My best friend is the world's most tolerant person. She has helped me view others without suspicion."

BETTY, 33: "Margaret is cautious where I am reckless. She's methodical, funny, reassuring and game for anything."

ORLA, 29: "My best friend is never shocked or disappointed in me."

JULIANNE, 40: "I see her so rarely, she is a gypsy. When we meet we love each other intensely and unconditionally. She is my mirror, soul sister and battery charger. I love my female friends. They are more raw and real than any other relationship."

CLAIRE: "Women do go to their friends and discuss their problems.... which men don't seem to be able to do. That starts in childhood. The thing is that little girls have little girl problems and when they share those problems with other little girls they don't feel so alone."

FIONA: "It's something I gain a tremendous amount of inspiration from. Female friendship is a life-line. Female solidarity is huge. Women are very good at being friends. I tell mine a lot about what's going on in my life. My being vulnerable around other women has helped them and me."

JEAN and **MAURA** like each other, a lot. They like each other so much they have formed a company together. And after working hours, they still socialise with each other

JEAN: "I think this is the first time that I have had a friendship with a woman where I am comfortable rowing. I was never confident in myself to go that far in a friendship.

"This morning we were having a discussion and we were absolutely disagreeing, but at the same time she was willing to see my point of view.

"Six years ago I thought she was a dizzy blonde bimbo. She was working with the same company as me at the time. Despite my prejudice we got friendly and started to spend more time together.

"We are very honest with one another, if I buy a dress Maura will say whether it looks awful. I don't think take offence from a friend who is frank. She is much more impetuous than I am, I try to calm her down!

"I always look forward to seeing her and when she is away I miss her.

"Working together and being friends... if there were going to be difficulties they would have manifested themselves very much at this stage. It can be problematic occasionally, because it is difficult to know where the friendship ends and the working relationship starts, and you have to be business-like in some sense or you might end up going off on a skite.

"We are a source of support for one another for other things that are going on in our lives. I talk to Maura an awful lot about my feelings, my emotions and I talk about problems I might be having with the kids to her all the time. She brings a steady influence to bear on it.

"I trust Maura 100%. I don't think she would misrepresent me in friendship or in our working relationship."

MAURA: "How did I manage to become friendly with somebody who thought I was a bimbo?.

"Actually Jean was somebody that looked terribly busy and important. I thought she took life far too seriously! Besides, she soon learned to stop judging by appearances.

"Our friendship is very solid and even. I can say or do anything and Jean is the same and there is no underlying agenda. Everyone is upfront and straight. If Jean gives me a stream of abuse I know there is nothing else behind it.

"Jean is, in a sense, a yardstick to measure things by. If I bounce something off Jean it comes bouncing back, with a different perspective, like 'I understand your point of view but listen to mine.' It gives you a sense of where you are in the world, it doesn't make it easier, but it certainly makes it more understandable."

Sisters

That 'yardstick' figures in this section too — not surprisingly since our sisters can also be our best female friends.

> *"Women who describe themselves as close to a sister, may talk about her as a 'mirror' or 'alter ego'. It relates to the age old fascination of the double. A sister's parallel life is a 'yardstick' or 'touchstone' — a constant point of reference from which she can gauge her own identity."*
> — BRIGID McCONVILLE 'Sisters'.

Whether you agree or not if you have a close sister you are very lucky. They are very precious. I have one. This is what she said about me, bless her:

AMANDA, 21: "My sister is there through thick and thin, she would be my closest and most reliable friend. She is a beautiful, compassionate, intelligent human being. If I say any more she will be too big-headed for words."

And I feel the same way about her. Nothing more to add to that.

DOREEN, 51: "My sister is part of my balancing act. I love her because she is not afraid to be honest."

And we won't get away without mentioning brothers:

BRID: "My big brother tells me about how men work and sizes up any man who comes near to make sure he won't hurt me. He doesn't say much but he is always there for me. He is 70 and I am 63."

SUZANNE, 28: "I had a strained relationship with my little brother in the past. The older we get the more tolerant we get of one another. My relationship with him is the only real, equal, platonic relationship I have with a man. He is so kind hearted."

The last word

The notion of learning to be yourself first, means you are not alone in any relationship — you have got you.

Over 100 women contributed to this publication. The section on relationships was the one which drew the biggest response. Here are some of the most telling and pertinent answers:

1. THE MOST IMPORTANT THING LISTED IN TERMS OF RELATIONSHIPS IS:

a. Trust
b. Love
c. Loyalty
d. Honesty
e. Passion
f. Friendship

2. WHAT DO THE WORDS 'BEING IN LOVE' MEAN TO YOU?

JENNIFER, 27: "Not needing to talk, a feeling of calm. Infidelity is not even considered, it would be preposterous."

BRYANA, 18: "An essential part of life."

ORLA, 30: "I'm not sure. I think I have been once...."

SINEAD, 20: "Trouble."

VIOLET, 29: "Someone you enjoy being with all the time but can give you space — and is good in bed!"

ORLA, 29: "Someone to share life with."

BETTY, 44: "Something to be treasured and let go when it wants to go."

BETTY, 33: "Making a complete tit of myself, being 'in like' is much better."

AMANDA, 21: "The initial phase of relationship when everything is rosey in the garden. If it makes it to the commitment stage you've got something special."

3. WHAT HAVE YOU GOT OUT OF A LONG-TERM RELATION-SHIP?

ORLA, 29: "I learned communication is very important and one can be very lonely living with someone."

AMANDA, 21: "Security, love, friendship, respect, happiness, trust."

ANNE, 23: "Someone I can relate to."

BETTY, 33: "Security, confidence, sex, various loans, but ultimately a bigger overdraft."

SINEAD, 37: "I have learned to compromise and see myself."

1. WRITE A LETTER

To the people you love most in your life, saying exactly why you care for them and expressing your hopes for the future which involve them. Even if you never send it, it will make you appreciate them. If you do send it you will have been responsible for making another human being happy.

2. TOP 12 INTIMACY NEEDS

This exercise comes courtesy of the Intimacy Therapy Centre.

Look over this list of needs. Mark your top three in order of importance - 1,2,3. Then do the same for what you perceive your partner's needs to be. This exercise can be done with any close friend too, if you want to explore your relationship further:

MYSELF	INTIMACY NEEDS	PARTNER
_____	ACCEPTANCE, accepting a person for what s/he is. Not trying to change her/him.	_____
_____	AFFECTION, showing care and closeness through physical touch.	_____
_____	AFFIRMATION, telling someone how great you think s/he is and pointing out strengths.	_____
_____	APPRECIATION, showing thanks for someone through words and actions.	_____
_____	APPROVAL, thinking and speaking well of someone	_____
_____	ATTENTION, conveying that you are listening to someone and interested in him/her.	_____
_____	COMFORT (EMPATHY), coming alongside someone with word, touch, understanding.	_____
_____	DISCIPLINE, helping someone to bring order to his/her life in a loving caring manner	_____

_____ ENCOURAGEMENT, urging someone _____
forward and gently persuading him/her toward
his/her personal goals.

_____ RESPECT, Valuing somebody, regarding _____
him/her highly, conveying to them their worth.

_____ SECURITY, Assurance of permanence of a _____
relationship.

_____ SUPPORT, Helping someone when s/he _____
needs it.

** Discuss with your partner why you have put your needs in this order, and why you
have put your partner's needs in a particular order. Then do the same with his/her list.
* Discuss how you and your partner can meet each other's primary needs.*

Further reading

We Two
by Roger Housden and Chloe Goodchild, Thorsons

Men are From Mars, Women are From Venus
by John Gray, Thorsons

Personal Relationships — Teenage Information Series
by Judy Greenwood, Chambers

Sisters
by Brigid McConville, Pan Books

Families and How to Survive Them
by John Cleese and Robin Skynner, TSP

Woman's Experience of Sex
by Sheila Kitzinger, Penguin Books

The Mirror Within
by Anne Dickson, Quartet Books

Chapter Six

~~~~

WHAT HAPPENED TO THE SUNSHINE?

"On the brightest, sunniest day of the year I was left wondering what happened to the sunshine in my soul." — CATHERINE

DEPRESSION CAN BE CAUSED and manifested in many different ways. But it has the same cumulative effect — absence of joy. The major depressive disorders require extensive psychiatric attention and usually medication, or other therapeutic interventions. Unfortunately they cannot be examined within the confines of this chapter. These depressions often arise for no discernible reason unlike what we call reactive depression. Reactive depression simply means reaction to life events and tragedy. 'What Happened to the Sunshine?' focuses on how reactive depression can stop you from *Being You*, living up to your true potential, how it hampers your ability to enjoy life.

If your particular experience of reactive depression in not included here it is only because the women interviewed had other reasons which caused their despair. It does not mean that your experience is any less valid.

According to recent surveys:

— 49% of Irish women will suffer with depression at some point in their lives*
— 16% of Irish women will be hospitalised with depression at some point in their lives*
— Women are twice as likely as men to be diagnosed as suffering from depression**
— Women are two to three times more likely to be prescribed tranquillisers**
(*Aware survey. **John of God's pamphlet.*)

These figures show if you are depressed you are not alone. Every second woman you pass on the street will feel the same as you do, or has done in the past, or will do in the future.

Here you can read the shared wisdom of wonderful women all either experiencing, helping, treating or living with those who feel an absence of joy in their lives.

MARIE MURRAY is Head of the Psychology Department in a major Psychiatric Hospital and a Clinical Psychologist and Psychotherapist. She has some valuable insights for us into the windowless world of the depression sufferer:

"I sometimes think it is a world where one looks through the window of life, from a dark and confined space and sees everyone else as being happy and successful and worthwhile. I remember a client once described it in this way: sitting in a small cave, behind a window through which she could see, but not be seen. Another person called it an abyss — dark, bottomless, where she had sunk so low she could only see a glimmer of light above.

"Others think of it as drowning, a slow suffocation of their energy and life."

Isolation

Depressed people always feel isolated, not part of the world, in their isolation their feeling of helplessness is magnified This is not helped by society's lack of understanding for their pain:

MARIE MURRAY: "The sense of isolation is often an acute feeling in depression, as if 'nobody understands my pain, nobody can see me and if they did they would turn away'. It is the great loss of self-esteem, self-worth and a sense of coping that makes depression such a lonely experience.

"With this isolation comes a great sense of fear, of hopelessness and helplessness — despair. When people feel real despair they need sensitivity. They need care. Remarks such as 'Pull yourself together', 'Count your blessings', or 'Stop thinking about yourself' can plunge a person further into depression. It does not jolt them out of it.

"People who are depressed can brood over what they view as past failures, present loss and bleak prospects. They need patience not pushing, love not lectures and they need — time."

MAE, 57: "I have suffered with cancer and I have suffered with depression and I can honestly say depression is worse. When I was a young married women I became agoraphobic. You get sympathy and support from the world when you have something visible like cancer. Depression is harder for people to understand.

"I could strangle people who say to depressed people 'Pull yourself together'. It is the most negative phrase and it imposes guilt on the sufferer. She feels like it is her fault, when she has every reason in the world to be happy and can't feel the joy. She counts the blessings in her life and feels she is not appreciating them.

"Don't try to come through it on your own. There are so many support groups, like Aware, available. You need to be able to share your experience with other people."

Loss

Depression can stem from lots of situations. A sense of loss is a key factor, loss of self-esteem or a sense of worth, loss of youth or fear of ageing, loss of employment or a role in life, loss of a partner through death or marital break-up, loss of hope or of dreams. People often talk about loss of self:

MARIE MURRAY: "I think the very Irish term 'I'm not myself' captures it beautifully. Treating depression is often about helping someone to find that self again, their value, their worth, their hope. Sometimes it's about creating a new self. As one woman said to me: 'I'm a new person — I don't know myself'."

Who defines women?

The way the world sees us can effect the way we see ourselves. We have to realise this societal pressure can contribute to feelings of depression. it's not easy to stand up for yourself when the world appears to ask women to do 10 things at once, without question. To question can be viewed as not coping. But we can never change without questions:

> **MARY**, 43: "They keep trying to put me into a box, a wife box, a worker box, a mother box...I wonder would they ever get lost and let me make my own box, that fits me?"

> **ELAINE**, 30: "I don't think there are many married women who get through life without getting depressed by what they have to cope with and how they are treated. A lot of women when they marry lose their identity. It doesn't do much for your self esteem. It doesn't help that society seems to think of you as 'Mrs So-and-So' instead of 'Individual with Separate Thoughts and Dreams.'
> "I've done a course in child care and it's given me the push I needed to look for respect. Soon I'll have the qualifications to work in a creche, or open one if I can. I don't feel as trapped as I used to. When you're trapped you turn on yourself because there's no-one else to turn on. That just makes you depressed."

One of the key questions in this chapter is how women are defined, determined, fitted into niches in our society:

> MARIE MURRAY: "How do we understand and interpret ourselves? Women have been given different roles at different times. During the war women were called on to work in services and ammunition factories. After the war they were advised to return home and be 'good mothers'.
> "Now women are confused about where they should be. I think it is unfortunate that women who choose to work at home often feel bad about themselves and their worth, while women who decide to work outside the home often feel guilty about this choice.
> "We need to ask ourselves — what is my choice? Why did I make it? Is it the best choice for me? If so, and nobody is harmed by your choice, stick with it. If not maybe it is time to review it."

Gentlemen — strong women:

> "This review does not just apply to women. Look at the way men have been constructed, as the providers, as the strong ones, as 'the head of the house'. Think how they feel when they have no work to let them be the 'provider', when they have no strength to be 'the strong one' and when all the ideas of 'head of the house' have been taken away.

Their roles are changing too. They are as confused as us:

MARIE: "As a therapist of 20 years I have come to the conclusion that there is no greater gentleness than that of a sensitive man and no greater strength than that of a strong woman. I think that men and women need to invite these qualities in each other. Men and women have the opportunities to take care of each other when either feels depressed."

Poverty

As we mentioned in the stress chapter — how do you treat depression if it is caused by situations out of your control? Those that have very little need help from the rest of us. Community groups are a vital resource anywhere, but especially in areas where poverty and unemployment are high, for these reasons:

MARIE MURRAY: "I have met women who have described themselves as depressed, and indeed they are sad, anxious, feeling overwhelmed and unable to cope, have poor sleeping and eating patterns, are irritable and feel unable to go on. But when I hear the story of their lives I know that if I had to live in their situation I would also be depressed.

"I know if I had six kids, no money, a husband who was angry (because of the world he has to live in) and the daily grind that they encounter I would not be sitting my side of the therapy room.

"I remember meeting a woman who kept saying to me, 'what do I need? Do I need therapy?' I remember thinking that she needed an extra £50 a week. It is so important for women to know sometimes that they are not 'mad' or 'crazy' but just stressed and struggling and surviving well in their situation. Many don't clinicians — they need cash."

PATRICIA, 32: "On Sundays we were reminded at mass 'Blessed are the Poor'. I didn't feel blessed. I grew up wanting never to be poor ever again, never to have to knock on the neighbour's door for a cup of something, never to have that feeling that you don't know where the next penny is going to come from, the insecurity. I am financially secure now yet I still feel that way.

"I will have that fear for the rest of my life, sometimes it overwhelms me. I get depressed thinking about all the people denied chances to progress in life because of financial and educational restraints. I feel guilty about not belonging with them anymore. So I deal with my depression through therapy and I try and help the people who need the breaks I was fortunate enough to have."

Seeking asylum

Hospitals are places of refuge and healing, 16% of Irish women will be hospitalised for depression. They are not 'mad', they are in need of help.

GERALDINE 50, is a woman who was given refuge in hospital when a number of difficulties overtook her and robbed her of the energy she needed to live:

"Before I became depressed a number of major events and tragedies happened in a two-year period. There had been bereavements, a car accident, my hysterectomy and my husband had a heart attack.

"He is also suffering from manic depression. Highs and lows. Medication has contained them, but there were years before diagnosis where things were hard going. He would spend money on shopping sprees and have grandiose ideas. There were times when I felt 'I can't take this'.

"After this hectic, awful two-year period I wasn't sleeping, waking early in the morning — which can be a symptom of depression. The doctor put me on an anti-depressant. He said that he could see it coming, that I was just punch drunk from everything. I couldn't cope any more, and I was checked into St. Patrick's Hospital.

"I felt terribly guilty, like I couldn't hold myself together, like I had no right to be depressed, like I really should have sought help earlier than I did. But I was so ill that I was glad to be hospitalised and not have to worry about everyone else.

"I found the time I spent in St Patrick's restored my energy and faith in myself. Just being able to step back from the responsibilities of my life made the recovery easier."

MARIE MURRAY: " I knew a woman who, when she felt really overwhelmed by it all, used to go to the psychiatrist and give all the symptoms of depression and suicidal intent. This was her way of getting a break, getting a little time in hospital. If she came from different social circumstances she would have a weekend in a hotel or a continental holiday, a bit of sun and recharging the batteries."

"Social conditions sometimes create the revolving door in psychiatric hospitals. The old word asylum was a good word because asylum means sanctuary, a safe place of refuge. For some people the psychiatric hospital serves the function of a place of refuge from the grim reality of their lives, for others it is a very necessary place for the treatment of serious disorder."

'Privilege'

While social conditions and poverty are big contributors to depression, studies show this does not confine feelings of depression to women in certain social situation and circumstance. I asked Marie about this:

"Depression is no respecter of social conditions or privilege. There are women who sometimes feel their identity is only seen through association with the 'important' identity of their partner.

"Their pain is equally deep. They cannot 'let themselves down' by talking about their feelings. They cannot pretend that anything ever goes wrong in their lives because that would implicate their partner and their position.

"They often talk to me about the energy they expend in trying to be perfect — perfect home, children, marriage, clothes. They are sometimes confronted by the question: 'Who am I in my own right?' Their sense of sadness is compounded by the fact that nobody has sympathy for them. They feel guilty because they have nothing to complain about. They cannot say 'I am down because I am hungry, tired, cannot pay bills.' But they need the same understanding: to be listened to, to be understood, to find themselves, to have their own worth and value."

SINEAD: "I know a woman who has a beautiful new car and her husband checks the mileage every week. It is not allowed over a certain amount. She has the finest of clothes, the best holidays and no freedom.

"She is depressed because she sees no way out. She will have nothing if she leaves. She is me. I can call me 'she' because I do not recognise myself as the woman I was before I married."

BRIDÍN TWIST, is president of the Irish Countrywomen's Association, **REGINA MARTIN** is a counselling psychologist working on the organisation's freephone helpline. Both women are from a rural background. They love the country way of life, but scratch the surface of the stereotypical rural idyll and you find very real problems. Rural women can have trouble hanging onto their identity in the male dominated world of farming:

REGINA: "There is a high incidence of suicide among farmers wives. They are among the highest figures in Ireland.

"Relationship problems between men and women are uppermost in the calls I deal with. 90% of my phone calls are from women complaining about their husband's lack of involvement in the marriage, or reluctance to provide adequate financial means for the family unit. Women marry the man, they marry the ethos, the status, the house and children. They marry the marriage.

"On the other hand men tend to have a more narrow view of their emotional responsibilities.

"If a woman is unhappily married on a farm, it's hard to sell up and move on. You are possibly looking at a four or five generation hold, and that ultimately creates a locked in position, for the woman in particular. Farms are rarely sold in marital breakups. That can create a huge amount of distress to women.

"If you marry a man who has been left a farm and you go into the marriage without your name on anything, then you are walking into trouble. You have to have agreements, even legal agreements, beforehand. The hand that holds the pen that signs the name at the bottom of the cheque book is the person who is ultimately in control.

"Basically what these women need to internalise, through therapy, is that they have permission to expect, and to have, a reasonable way of life. This may be hard to realise living in family units where male power is predominant.

"In my experience the women who have overcome stress/depression in rural areas have come from situations where they had no hope, and, through therapy, they acquired the skills and strategies to access their own hidden strengths. When a woman realises that there is absolutely nothing that she can't do, it is a wonderful day in her life."

BRIDÍN, grew up in a rural environment and throughout her life has seen the degree of isolation rural women, 40% of the Irish female population, live with. That isolation can lead to depression:

"The I.C.A. is a life-line for a lot of women in rural areas. In the case of many of our members the local guild will be the only outlet for them away from the farm. As one woman told me it was the only place in her life where she could put herself first.

"A lot of rural women are carers. They are the most unappreciated group of women. They are at home all the time with no one to relieve them. Just to give you an instance, I know one lady who looks after her elderly father-in-law and grown-up son with a disability. She runs a farm, with very little support systems in place.

"Farms are handed down from father to son traditionally so you will find very few women who will have control in that respect. Where does an elderly widow living on a farm go if her son/daughter and spouse break up and the property is divided between the couple? Where does she fit into the picture? She can feel very unwanted. That's bound to lead to depression.

"When the ICA movement was founded in 1910, by Horace Plunkett, it was looking at ways to improve women's lives in rural areas in particular.

"The same issues stand today. Isolation, poverty, depression. There is still not a lot of public transport for rural areas. Women are lucky if there is a car they have access to. You will find women who do not see anyone other than their families from one end of the week to the next.

"There are courses and clubs in place, but how to you access them if you have no transport system or childcare service?

"They were the two obstacles that came out in the second commission on the Status of Women, which our organisation was involved in. We surveyed our 26,000 members and we would have members out on the Aran Islands, as isolated as you could get. All women said the same thing: the fact that they could communicate with some other human beings was extremely important for them."

If you live in an isolated area join the ICA, they have many social events, classes and, most importantly, a freephone helpline.

Statistical 'breakdown'

We have quoted statistics in this chapter, just to show how widespread depression is. Behind each percentage and figure there are people suffering.

We need to help each other remove the shackles from our spirits. That can only happen through increased public awareness.

JULIE HEALY is National Support Group Co-ordinator — AWARE, she has devoted her life to increasing awareness about depression, trying to help people realise it is not a stigma but an illness.

She first encountered depression when her husband, Derek, was diagnosed as a manic depressive:

"I can understand why people don't want to admit to suffering with depression. In 1969 my husband Derek started to experience manic elations and depressions.

"I had read depression was caused by brucellosis! So I decided that's what Derek had — it sounded much more respectable than depression. He went and had tests but they showed negative for the brucellosis — obviously. So he was admitted to hospital for psychiatric evaluation.

"I totally denied it was happening, that something like that could happen to people like us. Now we try to help others so they don't feel the same way about depression."

Depression in the work place

It might cost the State an estimated £280 million per annum, with 200,000 depression suffers at any one time, but many newly diagnosed depression sufferers often think they will lose everything by admitting it openly. They can think they might lose their jobs. This is not the case.

JULIE HEALY: "My husband's firm are aware of his illness. I know it can be very difficult to admit you are depressed, particularly at work.

"But if you are suffering from depression and finding it hard to cope at work it is very difficult to hide this from an employer. It is also very difficult for people to work up the courage to speak to an employer. But you really are better off handling your own PR rather than let rumours take a life of their own. There will be rumours because it is nearly impossible to keep something like that secret. People will be uncomfortable if they're not supposed to know.

"Depression is not a rare illness. A lot of my work, as a relative of a sufferer and an Aware worker, is to change public perception of depression. When I go into schools I ask the children to guess how many people will suffer from depression during their lives. They very rarely guess the figures are so high."

ELAINE, 25, has lived and battled with depression on and off for years:

"I was working in a terrible factory job. It was inhumane — the managers were bad and the conditions and pay worse. A number of personal problems came up around the same time and I found I just couldn't cope anymore. I felt trapped by my life, as if this was all I was ever going to be and all I could expect. I never spoke about my problems or shed a tear. I just withdrew into my own world. I thought it was normal to feel miserable and alone.

"When I found I could not physically get up for work in the morning I went to the doctor for a cert. He said he thought that I needed psychiatric help. I came out and fell around the place laughing, I think out of fear, because it was official, I was off the wall. Looking back I can't get over how bad I was.

"They put me on medication and referred me to a psychiatrist. He was in his late 60s and I nearly ran out when I first saw him, wondering what an old man could do to help me.

"It ended up that I went to him for six months. I felt great talking to him.

"I didn't think that anyone would want to look at me or talk to me.

"I came to realise it was not normal to cry all the time and feel inadequate. If someone gave me a present I would wonder why, and what they wanted from me. I thought that I wasn't good enough for someone to like because I was useless and worthless. I've been in the depths, I wouldn't say I'm on a high now, but I do have a light at the end of the tunnel. I can say now, 'I feel lousy today, I'll have a cry and tomorrow it'll be different.' The antidepressants I took for six months had me floating around from day to day. They helped me to do the basic things like getting out of bed and washing myself, to go through the motions of living.

"But the talking was what really helped. Talking reaches the soul."

Childbirth

SHEILA, 30, suffered severe post natal depression, was hospitalised and treated for it. On release she found the support of her local family resource centre to be invaluable:

"About three months after the birth of my third child I got sick and started to suffer with panic attacks. I lost all my energy and did not know what was wrong with me. I went to my doctor who told me I was a good healthy girl and to get a good night's sleep. I couldn't sleep. I started knocking on strangers' doors telling them to bring me to hospital, because I thought I was dying. Because I couldn't sleep I didn't have the energy to even carry the baby.

"My mother ended up taking him from me and I went to another doctor who, thankfully, saw what was wrong with me straight away. He told me it was postnatal depression. I was sent to see a psychiatrist.

"He said 'You should be in hospital'. I was so glad somebody cared. I kept apologising because I was actually filthy, I did not have the energy even to wash my hair.

"My main worry when they sent me to hospital was my little boy who was sick. They couldn't have been nicer about it, they gave me a little room with a cot in it and he came with me to hospital. I never went anywhere without him. I was in for three months.

"As soon as I got my physical strength back I checked myself out because my other children were fretting for me. I was only home two weeks when my heart started pumping again and I felt like my insides were going to fall out. I lost control of my breathing.

"I came up to my family resource centre and the nun who ran it, Sr Bernadette, took one look at me and said 'Sheila, I want you to promise to come up here every day.' I did, the other women took care of the baby for me and I just sat in the centre every morning, often not doing anything, just feeling secure. I had company and support. In the afternoon I had strength to carry on myself.

"Then I did a personal development course. At first I wouldn't say anything in front of strangers but I did end up sharing things. The confidentiality was never broken — there was a bond between us all. I remember telling them about looking at my children and saying to myself: 'I can't rear you, I can't mind you.' I know now I am a good mother and things just got on top of me. We talked about our health, our financial problems, our feelings. There were lots of tears and arguments too. But the bond was there and the bond helped me get well again."

MARIE MURRAY: "Women are sold the picture postcard of tranquil mother and sleeping cherub and feel very guilty if they are simply ragged, holding a howling baby. I think that it is important for women to admit to each other that those early days are very hard work, that after the elation of giving birth they are also tired, that no sleep in the night can make you feel frayed and this does not make you a bad mother. Babies often take time to adjust to the world so they cry to signal their needs not their disappointment in our mothering, not their rejection of us.

"It is sad that women would feel angry with, or rejected by, their babies when what is really happening is two lives are adjusting to each other. Again, if we ask how women are socially constructed around childbirth, it is very difficult for them to admit to feeling depressed at what is meant to be the happiest times."

Childhood memories

In an ideal world we would all like to think every child was loved and nurtured. Some are not. **LAURA**, 36, carried the pain of childhood until a women's group allowed her to release it:

"I spoke to concerned and caring women about the things I have kept locked up since childhood. I had a safe haven and I opened up the old wounds — it was painful but to keep them closed was destroying me. My father left when I was very young and my mother blamed us children. It left a lot of scars.

"I got all the support I needed from the women I was sharing my past with. I cried from my heart and I felt all the hate melted tear by tear. Hearing the traumas other women have experienced helped.

"For years I had to be big, strong, the hard woman, just to survive. Deep down I wasn't the hard one. Now I can cry for that little child I want back. I want to nurture her like I nurture my own, very precious, beautiful children. I can put myself back to being seven and I can listen to her. Pain can be dealt with and accepted. What would I say to other women? To share is to grow and to grow is to survive."

Finding hope

For those of us who have experienced depression, who feel depressed right now, it is hard to find any reason to feel hopeful. Yet this is what all the women who talked to me felt and feel — they have found, through reaching out, the hope they needed. They want you to feel the same as they do, to acknowledge the rightful place of your pain in your heart and to realise it has a role — to deepen your understanding of life and to help you to a realisation of yourself. It is a cry for help — don't ignore it.

The Aware Helpline is listed in the directory. Someone will listen if you call it. No-one is going to dismiss your feelings. As you will realise from MARIE MURRAY's last words:

"I admire so many of the people I work with and how they reclaim their lives. They get better. Being a therapist is an enormous privilege. You are invited into the lives of others at their deepest and most profound moments. You are being entrusted with their pain. Depression is personal for those who experience it, it is not just a clinical entity. Therapy is not just a clinical encounter, it is a human encounter."

Would you recognise depression?

This Aware questionnaire will help you realise if you are suffering with depression. If you have had any of the following symptoms for more than two weeks consult your GP:

Are you feeling persistently sad, anxious or do you have an empty feeling?

Are you tired or slowed down, despite rest?

Have you lost interest in food, sex, work?

Are you wakening during the night, too early in the morning or having trouble getting to sleep?

Have you lost (without dieting) or gained weight?

Are you having difficulty thinking, remembering or making decisions?

Are you feeling guilty or worthless?

Have you been having thoughts of death or suicide?

Do you have aches or pains without physical cause?

Further reading

Feeling Good
by David M Burns M.D.
Signet

Coping with Depression and Elation
by Dr. P McKeon
Sheldon Press

Depression and its Treatment
by John Griest, James W Jefferson
Contact Aware for details
147 Phibsborough Road
Dublin 7

Your Erroneous Zones
by Dr Wayne W. Dyer
Sphere

Lithium, A Practical Guide
by Dr P McKeon, Dr S O'Brien, Dr J Fehily
Aware publication

Notes on Depression
by Dr P McKeon, Mrs G Corcoran
Aware publication

Mental Illness — A Family Affair
Dr. Martina Corry
Aware publication

Aware Magazine
147 Phibsborough Road
Dublin 7

How to Heal Depression
by Dr Harold H Bloomfield & Peter McWilliams
Thorsons

Chapter Seven

~~~~

GOODBYE

WOMEN INVEST SO much in caring and nurturing others that 'goodbye' is a word which brings us great pain. In the relationships chapter women talked about children leaving home and marriages breaking down, here they talk about bereavement.

We know that separation, death, moving on and growing apart are all facts of life and we will experience one, if not all, in a lifetime.

The parting of ways can leave great gaping holes in the self and the expert and women who talk of their experience in 'Goodbye' have all come to terms with that and have filled them as best they can.

NOLEEN SLATTERY is a bereavement counsellor who works with everyone from children to pensioners. She explains that grieving over a death brings a change of identity and a challenge to learn how to be who you are now, without the loved one's physical presence:

"Grieving over a death is depression, you cannot separate the two except to say that with grief at least you know the cause of your feelings lie in bereavement. It is so painful and everyone's experience of it differs.
— When you lose someone close to you:
— You feel down.
— You have nightmares, you tremble.
— You feel ill, with insomnia, extreme tiredness, headaches, chest pains, palpitations and many more.

— You feel anger, which arises from a wide variety of feelings, beliefs and situations.
— You feel isolated, you don't want to meet people, or socialise anymore.
— You feel frustrated, not fully understanding what's happened to you and not being listened to.
— You feel alone, isolated, you feel different.
— You feel sad, either crying all the time or wanting to cry.
— You feel confused.
— You worry about money, the financial implications are often not realised until someone has passed on.
— You feel fear, for the future. Suddenly you have to think about life insurance, emergency needs, pensions, paying off loans at a time when you feel least able to deal with them.
— You feel guilty in that you could have cared more or loved better.

— You might feel all these things in one day or you might feel only one of them. They are normal reactions.

"If you go for counselling you will be listened to in a way the rest of the grieving family might not be able to listen. You have an appropriate listener, non-judgmental and accepting, able to hear the bad and the good. You will learn it is OK to feel whatever you feel. Do not be afraid of anger. Do not try to go through bereavement alone.

"Children in particular suffer terribly dealing with bereavement — they haven't got the knowledge and vocabulary to deal with the spectrum of emotions they are going through. I have counselled children who have turned against the living parent because they believe he or she loves love the deceased more than them. I have worked with children who are afraid to let the remaining family members leave the house in case one of them dies.

"For any bereaved person there is no set period for recovery — individuals come to terms with death of a loved one at their own pace.

"I advise people not to do anything for a year, because you can behave very irrationally. I've known people who have redecorated their house from top to bottom, at enormous expense, but the pain is still inside them.

"The most disturbing deaths have to be suicides — where the family feel a burden of incredible guilt and disbelief that someone so close to them could take their life. It literally rips them apart inside. They will have questions that they will never know the answers to. It's important to help them understand the dead person made a personal choice, they are not to blame. That person was responsible for his or her own life."

Losing a child

Losing a child is a huge thing to cope with. A life has not been lived to the full and there is always the notion of 'never enough time', you never had enough time with them and they never had enough time to do the things they would have done.

MOIRA, 46, lost her 12-year-old son, MICHAEL, over a year ago, in a tragic road accident:

"I'm grieving for him, he was my baby. So now I am finished rearing my children. All of a sudden, without warning.

"I don't feel angry against the driver, he wasn't drunk, he wasn't reckless, Michael wasn't murdered, it was an accident.

"I wouldn't have any advice for any other mother but to say, talk to yourself, listen to yourself, that is what I do when I am sitting on my own. Feel the pain, you have to feel it, don't be afraid of the memories.

"I have spoken to people who have lost a child, and they can't bear to look at photographs, can't bear to go into a room, that hasn't happened to me, I have Michael's photographs everywhere in the house.

"Michael was loved by everyone, so his friends are grieving too. We had a barbecue for all his little pals, to celebrate his life not his death, because those children could not understand what had happened, all the neighbours and friends came and helped.

"Then the following week I put all his things on the kitchen table, I kept certain things back for myself and the children chose something they wanted belonging to Michael. Those children felt robbed too. It is a terrible lesson for children of 12 to learn, that they are mortal, they were so confused and frightened by it all.

"I have a box with all his little writings and all his little cards, all the little things about his life, he loved poetry, although his pals weren't to know that. I thought I could part with that box, when it came up to his first anniversary, but I couldn't. There was a side to Michael that only I knew.

"I don't know what it will be like next year, but I can't be afraid. You can busy yourself all you want but it is still there when you go to bed at night and it is still there in the morning, you just have to learn to live with it. The only way I can look after him now is to go and tend his grave.

"The only consolation is that he will never experience heartbreak, disappointment, drug abuse, sexual abuse, unemployment. He had the best years of his life, the fun years, no responsibilities, he died as he lived, fast, so thank God for that. He gave me so much joy and I can't negate that joy by thinking of all I am not going to have from Michael in the future."

Rituals

The ritual of a funeral is very important. You are saying goodbye to someone you loved and that is very important. You only realise how important it is when you meet people who have lost someone who has gone missing. And when someone disappears without trace you can never get to grieve properly, even though you know there is a very little hope of them being alive you can never really put them to rest.

JUDITH, lost ANNA two days after she was born:

"She is everywhere in the house, we can all feel her. At birth she had sustained such massive brain damage she only lived for two days.

"We kept Anna at home with us. We did what we needed to do. We blessed her. Two days later we organised the funeral. I was so lucky that I had the presence of mind and spiritual awareness to be able to use that time. Even though it was heartbreakingly sad it as a huge lesson in so many things.

"I think because we had the opportunity to have some control — keeping her at home — we were able to say goodbye to her in the way that made it more easy to come to terms with her death. We grieved immediately. I felt forlorn for months but I never spiralled into deep depression. When people go through bereavement, if they have had hard times before, it can be so hard to recover. But if I was to describe myself I would say I was fairly happy and reasonably balanced.

"And there were reminders everywhere — things I had bought. I was also dealing with a body that had just given birth. The milk came. It was the most cruel thing and I think mothers who have lost babies at birth just don't talk about that. I had a very sweet and practical mother-in-law who tore up a sheet and tied me so the milk was suppressed as much as possible — for 10 days it was really unpleasant."

A framed picture of Anna sits in the hallway — 10 x 12 inches — she is a beautiful baby, with a shock of black hair and a half-smiling expression — the family call her the resident Angel.

JUDITH: "I thought that there would never be a day when I wouldn't cry. But all the cliches that people use come into play as truth. Time heals. Life goes on. You can't stop — I can remember at the funeral at the graveside Daniel, my six-year-old, wanted me to run off and play tag with him. I did. I had to follow life. Playing tag at Anna's funeral... Daniel helped me so much to get over it.

"It was really hard to let go of her. So hard. Her spirit is still with us. Six months later I got pregnant with Jack and the rest is history! He is the most talkative, energetic little boy."

Partner's death

Coming to terms with a partner's death is whole new learning process. If you have lived in a good partnership it's very difficult to come to terms with being single again. Most people in this position are older and they have a lifetime of memories and companionship built up with and around the person who died. They are now alone, without them.

> NOELEEN: "The most important thing about going through the grieving process is to look after yourself, you have to remain aware of yourself or your needs get lost in the pain of adjustment
> — Look after the basic needs:
> — eat a little, to keep your strength
> — drink plenty of water to stop you dehydrating from crying
> — sleep, and if you cannot sleep, rest and don't feel pressurised to sleep
> — be easy on yourself."

OLIVE, 57, found the traditional Irish wake helped her greatly in coming to terms with the death of her husband, Paddy, a few years ago:

"The country way of saying goodbye is a good way. It's the way Paddy would have wanted.

"They came from the four corners of Ireland and abroad, for three days there was never less than 100 people here. The neighbours came in and made tea and sandwiches and drinks. They stayed up all night, we all did, you don't go to bed. The parish priest came up and said the Rosary before the removal. One man who Paddy hadn't seen for 30 years came up and put his arms around me and recalled a greyhound bitch Paddy trained. That got me through it, to know he was so loved by family and friends.

"You can't go to a funeral parlour and sit there all day, when the body is at home in an open coffin you can see the deceased all you want.

"When the wake ends and the guests leave it hits you — you are alone. But being brought up in the country helps, I've been attending wakes since a child and there is no better way to say goodbye, let me tell you that. The country people don't forget a widow. The neighbours are the salt of the earth — even now they know I miss him and they talk about him.

"At a wake people talk about years past and other people who have left this world. It helps you realise there are others going through it every minute of the day, every day of the week. Death is part of life and living."

Stages of grief

Clearly a bereaved person finds themselves in a very stressful, painful situation. If we can understand their needs we should be able to develop pointers as to the best sort of counselling and skills to use. Listen to what the bereaved person wants and support them.

PAIN
"Grief is painful, and I believe this pain is part of healing so I try not to encourage its numbing with pills, sleeping pills should only be taken if the bereaved person wants them. They need to be allowed to suffer and to express their grief in whatever way is appropriate to them."

LONELINESS
"The bereaved person may feel abandoned and lonely, in need of physical comfort, such as a hug or arm around the shoulder."

MEMORIES
"People want to remember the person who has died. Often the bereaved say that friends and relatives won't allow them to talk about the deceased when this is what they want to do."

ANGER
"There may be a lot of anger towards the dead person. There may be often so-called unacceptable emotions and these should be allowed to be expressed."

LISTENING
"Bereaved people have a great need to be listened to. Experts identify clear stages which the emotions have to pass through for bereavement to be complete. These are Denial, Isolation, Anger, Depression and Acceptance. The bereaved need to be guided through them, through counselling so they can experience these emotions without guilt."

Further reading
Facing Death
by Averil Stedford
Heinemann, 1984

All the End is a Harvest
by Agnes Whittaker
Darton, Longman and Todd, 1984

Chapter Eight

~~~~

MY BODY IS BEAUTIFUL

"A woman is often measured by the things she cannot control.
She is measured by the way her body curves or doesn't curve,
by whether she is fat or straight or round.
She is measured by 36-24-36 and inches and ages and numbers -
by all the outside things that don't ever add up to who she is on the inside.
if a woman is to be measured, let her be measured by things she can control
by who she is and who she is trying to become. Because, as every woman knows, measurements are
only statistics and statistics lie." — Nike Advert

WHEN WE LOOK IN THE MIRROR, what do we see? Hair, eyes, ears, nose, cheeks, mouth, neck, shoulders, arms, hands, breasts, waist, stomach, hips, pubic hair, thighs, knees, calves, feet, toes among other bits. That is it — your body. The body you were born with, developed, abused, hid, dressed up, pampered, moisturised, made up, fed, dieted, cried over and exercised.

Welcome to your body. It's time to start feeling good about what you've got.

Surveying over 100 women for this book I asked them two simple questions about their body: How they feel and what was their favourite/worst bit? Not one woman's answer involved the most obvious parts of her feminine shape — breasts and buttocks. But most of the advertising, diet and exercise regimes are focused on toning up, pumping up or pushing up these parts of our anatomy.

Here's a selection of answers to the two questions:

HOW DO YOU FEEL ABOUT YOUR BODY?
"A bit worried, actually."
"When it's in shape — fine."
"It depends on my mood."
"I am very happy with the body I have. It has taken me a while to accept it mainly because of external, negative influences. I would like if it could be a bit smaller and fitter. I'm working on that too."
"I like it."
"I hate it."

"I'd like to change parts if it was possible without surgery — legs, feet, stomach, bum..."
"The basics are good. But I don't look after it at all. I haven't got a good figure. But if I pick the right clothes I look OK."
"It's OK."
"Sometimes I hate it, especially when these skinny-malinky fashions are in vogue. I'm

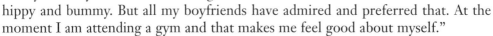

hippy and bummy. But all my boyfriends have admired and preferred that. At the moment I am attending a gym and that makes me feel good about myself."
"I am amazed at its stamina and resilience. I am slightly detached from its shape — are my tits really that long? What has happened, over the years, to my labia?"
"Sometimes good. Usually not good."
"Sometimes I feel grand about it, other times I feel crap about it. Mostly I feel I could lose a few pounds and get fit. Mostly I do nothing about that."
"Depends on my time of the month."
"I have no major problem with my body. I am unhappy with my tendency to put on weight."
"I used to hate my body. Since I had my baby two months ago I like it. I appreciate now what my body is capable of doing. It carried and can now feed another human being. I have a stretch mark too and I like it."
"I'm not disgusted with myself."
"Pretty good. Exercise has helped."

WHAT IS YOUR FAVOURITE/WORST PART?
"My face is nice."
"My tastebuds!"
"My eyes and legs are grand."
"My eyes and hair are my favourites."
"My smile, my mother says it could do the job of a lighthouse."
"I like my waist and the colour of my eyes."
"I like my height and my eyes. I hate my chin."
"I think my legs could be insured for a million, the rest would fetch about 50p."
"I love my feet. I watched them carry me, shoeless, in deserts, over mountains and they are so little! They make me cry."
"My eyes and my femininity, the rest I'm not so sure of."
"My eyes."
"My mouth is my best bit. It talks me out of situations and into others."
"My wrist is the only normal part of me."
"My back is smooth as glass with a lovely curve."

"My eyes and my legs are good, my face. I hate the fat on my torso."
"I hate my ears, they stick out, they're too big. Don't tell anyone I said that. They will start noticing them again."

"I have good legs and nice blue eyes."
"God knows what my favourite part is. I don't like my legs or belly much."
"My feet. Because they are so sensitive and they respond well to TLC. Also they never put on weight."

It's official as far as 100 of us, ranging in age from 18 to 70, are concerned — Irish women's favourite physical attributes are the 'windows of the soul" — their eyes. Without realising it these women have got the whole idea of body image and how to improve it, in the palms of their hands. They have chosen the part of their body which expresses their inner selves the most. The eyes will tell you more about a person than anything else. A few others chose aspects which allow them to express themselves — their mouths and their smiles.

The parts they hate most centre around the areas which accumulate fat deposits and receive bits of media attention. Nobody writes features on how to tone up your eyes and smile. These are the parts of us that are allowed to be free and function without fashionable influence or dictate. The unquantifiable parts. The unmeasurable. The thing now is to help the rest of our physiques enjoy that liberty.

JUDITH ASHTON is a woman who works on awareness and self-development through massage and psychotherapy. She has run body image workshops in different parts of the country and is now based in Kilkenny.

"I now take it as a foregone conclusion that you rarely meet a person with a very positive, complete acceptance of their body, and even though most people would be normal, and present as normal, with no major disfigurements or scars or handicaps or whatever, everybody would have a body image issue.

"Generally people with a good body image have worked on themselves on some level, whether that would be psychologically to get to the point of acceptance or perhaps physically through things like exercise, yoga, massage. That gives them some feel of control of their body image. They have decided to do something about themselves.

"Still, it is very rare to meet somebody who would like themselves 100%. Sometimes I am amazed at the type of things that people would have hang-ups about. I had a woman once who was really gorgeous, her image problem was her ears.

"I looked to see if she'd had ears like a bat or something, but they were OK. She was going to have an operation to have them pinned back, and when I saw her again after the operation I couldn't actually see the difference, but she was happier. She had had this issue about her ears and in a way I thought it was very sad."

How many of the women Judith has worked with would have contemplated cosmetic surgery?

"Quite a lot. I know of one woman who was very fit , she was a tennis player, enjoyed aerobics, golf. So she had a really fit body. She had her breasts made bigger for her husband's birthday present. I am continually appalled and saddened at the lengths people go to, to get a feeling of being accepted, and behind all that how much did this woman accept herself?"

"It seems we are encouraged to fight or ignore the different phases our bodies go through as part of the growth, maturing and ageing process. Then, of course, there is the stereotypical body image that women want to attain."

Your body changes, your hair greys, gravity pulls, you start to sag. We do not reach 70 looking like a 21 year-old, no matter how much surgery or exercise we do. But our society is set up to deny that, to turn back the clock. We're really denying who we are if we don't accept our bodies:

JUDITH: "One of the things that I would impress on people is if you have a good body attitude your energies should be flowing correctly, if you have a negative body image then the energy is not flowing properly through that area. It seems to me that very often people will get problems in areas that they are not so very happy with. So it's important to accept what you have.

"When the women come into the body image workshop they can expect to start loving the bit of them that they hate, or at least start liking it. It's a good sign if they attend a course in the first place.

"Very often body image problems have a historical basis. Somebody has said at some point that they did not like those parts of your body. When you look at what women have done to alter their body images — wasp waists, bound feet, corsets, pointed shoes that don't let the foot breathe, six-inch heels to get to a certain height, it can make you angry to see the pain women have endured to become more attractive.

"Look at the whole commentary around our breasts. It doesn't matter what size they are in terms of the job they are designed to do. You can have small breasts and feed adequately or large breasts and feed adequately. I think a lot of the problems people have with breast-feeding has nothing to do with the size of their breasts. They have simply been made to feel inadequate about them."

MAIREAD, 49: "I didn't breast-feed because I didn't feel capable of it. I never had what you would call a chest, a proper chest. Now I wish I had breast-fed. I would have liked to have used them for what nature intended."

In Judith's experience very often what stops people coming to terms with their body image is other people. It's very hard to come to terms with stretch marks if your husband is saying "I hate those stretch marks", these are contour lines on the map of your life experience. Each scar and mark has a story to tell about you. They belong to you.

JUDITH: "I would say 80% of my clients would not show their scars. These are scars after operations such as mastectomy, hysterectomy, colostomy. I advise them, if they are psychologically able and many are not when the first come to see me, to go home and stand in front of the mirror naked and just look. Look at what that scar says to you. You went through a painful operation and came out the other side. You have strength and you got through it.

"It seems no matter how intelligent and beautiful we are, no matter how much we have achieved and will continue to achieve, we can never be happy with our bodies. It does not seem to matter how many people tell us we are beautiful physically. We can have all the love in the world and still not feel it:

NOREEN, 53, is size 16/18. She has a beautiful face, blonde hair, is well dressed and groomed, has a great sense of humour, a thriving career and a loving family. She has done a lot of personal development work. But she is unable to love her body completely. It's almost as if it's the final frontier of acceptance, for her and many other women:

"It's the whole business too of never really feeling good enough, the sense of always feeling too fat, too small, wearing glasses, never feeling beautiful, you know? Why do I feel like this? I mean I am not exactly Brigitte Bardot but on the other hand I am not exactly painful to the eyes either. I am saying that in my head, but in my heart and in my body I'm feeling profoundly not good enough

"No matter what you do with yourself you are still not really right.

"You keep getting thinner, you keep doing this to your hair and that to your teeth and so on. It's like trying to get an explanation. The quest to like myself and my body has led me into all kinds of corners and all kinds of interesting places in terms of feminist thought and writing. But it's an ongoing process."

ROSEMARY KHALIFA, is a body harmony therapist and teacher. She helps people get in tune with their bodies in the deep, spiritual sense. From having experienced a severe dislike of her form she has learned to love her body, and now devotes her time to sharing that love with others, men and women.

For her the body is something that cannot be categorised, yet we attempt to do this continually. We use words like slim, trim, tidy, pert, neat, toned, to describe something that is not really any of those things. To be female is to have curves, flowing lines, fat, a unique shape. There are thousands of variations on the theme of physical femininity.

Rosemary believes you also store all your past experiences in your body, in that unique form, so to cope with them you have to be in tune with it:

"Body harmony is a hands-on therapy, it works on the premise that throughout your life you deal with trauma and it lodges in your body and becomes a body secret. You have to find a safe space to let that those secrets go.

"When people have a lot of trauma stored you'll see it in their posture — chest held in, shoulders rounded, the hips will be tight, the shoulders and neck tight. I find myself watching people walk. A lot of Irish people don't walk properly. Held back from their true potential is the description I would use.

"Sexuality is a huge issue for Irish women. When you have not explored your sexuality your whole self-esteem and who you are is blocked and the body reflects this. Repression can lead to lots of physical complaints.

"Most of the people I treat don't like some aspect of themselves. If we are negative about ourselves how can we hope to be positive about our bodies? We have conditions attached to almost everything so we will have conditions about our bodies. 'I'll lose weight and then I'll be happy', 'When I wear my wonderbra I look more sexy', 'When I've got my clothes on I am alright'.

"What about when the clothes are off? Naked is how you were born, naked is who you are. In your nakedness is your true essence.

"Massage is a good way of coming to terms with your body, warts, wonderful parts and all. If you don't have the money to treat yourself on a regular basis then you can go to an evening class and swap massages with other women. You can buy a book and read it with your partner. Massage is not just about sex, it is about giving your body loving attention.

"Kids have natural body harmony, they haven't been conditioned. They have natural body posture, they haven't started carrying body secrets. And all children are beautiful. As are all adults.

"Tactile and sensory treatment is wonderful for enhancing your self-esteem around the body. I don't know many people who hate being hugged, although I do treat people who are afraid of hugs."

So there you have it, the next time your mother/sister/friend/aunt/niece/granddaughter/daughter/cousin is moaning about her size and shape, don't raise your eyes to heaven and wonder what the hell she's talking about. Put your arms around her, tell her she is beautiful.

Then, hopefully in your self-hate moments she will do the same for you. Or, better still, you can do it for yourself.

Beauty

It might also be helpful to know that not all gorgeous women are happy in their physiques. For instance, tall, gorgeous women can have nowhere to hide, they will never blend into the background like us mere mortals. If they take up modelling it can put the spotlight on their looks even more. Their personalities get buried beneath a pile of foundation and bright studio lights.

ELEANOR, 25, is 6 foot two inches, and stunning looking. She is a horribly nice and sickeningly considerate creature with brains to burn. She eats chips, dessert and other normal, tasty things. She modelled for a time and now works in television where she is carving out a successful career as journalist and presenter:

"Like most women, that there are things about myself that I'd like to change, but by and large I'm happy with my body, but I think all the usual things like my bottom and hips are too big.

"Growing up I was really self-conscious about it and I got slagged and called names like: 'Mammy Long-Legs 'and 'Lanky' and 'Your Mother told you not to be long' and things like that. I'd say I only got really got comfortable with my height when I was around 18 or 19. When I was young, I was really self-conscious about my height and was very uncomfortable about it. I had little or no success with boys — they were all so small!

"I've become a lot more confident since then, because I've grown up a bit more. Like it or lump it — this is the way I am.

"It is an asset — sometimes. It does get you noticed — that can be good or that can be bad. One of the advantages is I find very few men intimidating. It's great to be able to talk to men at their eye level.

"The one thing my mother drilled into me was to walk straight because when you're very tall — you're always inclined to stoop — purely so you can hear people a lot of the time! It's because of my mother that I walk straight.

"For a very short while I modelled. At first it was great fun and it probably gave me a little bit more confidence and it was extra cash. It was good fun, putting on make-up and getting dressed up. But after a while I didn't like it

"I was having a laugh, going out with all my friends at night, eating junk food and things like that. I was studying in college and I knew what I wanted to do when I left.

"But, I'd never been in an environment before where you were judged purely on how you looked, what weight you were, how clear your skin was, how good your hair was.

"When you went in you had to stand on a weighing scales and be weighed. Then were told to lose weight, told 'You wore those clothes the last time you were in, and maybe you should wear something different the next time.'

"I just hated it.

"I decided it was far too much like hard work, and that there were a lot more important things to worry about, than whether you're one-stone overweight or half-a-stone overweight. I just didn't think it was important enough. Maybe, if I'd wanted to make a living out of it I would have made more of an effort, but I just liked my lifestyle too much. I still do and I wouldn't sacrifice food for anything."

CLAIRE, 32, on the other hand, is five-foot nothing:

"I was always the baby Jesus in school plays. I was too small to be taken seriously. Now that I look a lot younger than 32 I like it. But can you imagine what it was like never being served in pubs, always being treated like a baby? It was like I was never allowed to grow up.

"I've carried that into my adult life. I very much like to be taken seriously. There is no doubt in my mind that your outer appearance can effect the way people treat you and I've had to work very hard against that. I feel now I'm coming into my own. Because I am small it's hard to pin an age on me and consequently it's hard to label me."

Physical illness

When you suffer from any debilitating condition it is even more vital to love and care for your body. You're not fighting against it, you're fighting with it.

MAE, 57, chairs the breast cancer, self-help group Reach to Recovery. When she had her mastectomy she found it changed her whole way of thinking about life, and herself:

"Before, my life was devoted to home, family and little else, after cancer that all changed.

"The lump was just in the centre to the right of my left breast, at the cleavage more or less. In those days they did the full mastectomy. Basically, you think it is never going to happen to you, so when it happens you can flop or you can grab life by the throat and say 'I have a second chance and I am going to enjoy it'.

"The first thing I did was enrol in swimming classes, then I said yes to every opportunity that came my way. That included getting in touch with Reach to Recovery about 18 months after my mastectomy. I got such strength from that. Although you don't think about it, you are looking for a reason as to why it happened. Working as a counsellor you feel 'This is why it happened, it was so that I could do this important work.' Most of the women in Reach To Recovery have found that cancer changed their lives and priorities. They gain confidence from coming through the illness and have learned to put themselves first.

"The appearance of mastectomy is not actually that unsightly. You are simply flatter on one side than the other. It is very sore and tender at first and there is a scar afterwards. I certainly never hid my scar from my husband. It is a part of me and who I am.

"I know it helped that I had reared my children and was not going to be pregnant again. Some women I counsel have problems if they are not in a long-term relationship or if their partner can't handle it.

"I know loads of beautiful, glamorous women who have had mastectomies, double mastectomies and lumpectomies. The reconstruction surgery is so good and the prosthesis are very good too. Also the lingerie and clothing for women who have had mastectomies is really gorgeous. There is no reason to feel ugly and unattractive. I can honestly say I feel more attractive now, at 57, than ever."

Arthritis

Arthritis affects far more men then women. **VERONICA CANNING** is Chief Executive of the Arthritis Foundation of Ireland, she has found that many people with arthritis find it hard to feel good about their bodies:

"Your body image can be distorted when viewed through a veil of pain. Simple things become quite difficult, like standing or sitting up straight. It can be hard to wash, dress, put on jewellery.

"The pain can be low-grade but constant — always nagging away at your well-being and diminishing your quality of life. It can be so strong it takes over your whole life at times.

"Looking good and feeling good are intertwined. So it's all the more important when you have arthritis to enhance your body image. We've just published a book on exercise for those with arthritis called *Move it or Lose It*, since exercise is such a vital part of physical well-being. We suggest to our members if they can't get out to shop for new outfits they try catalogues. We have a mail order system for aids and appliances to help you to put on tights, close buttons — even brush your hair."

Belly dancing — the key to internal beauty

Belly dancing is one good way of appreciating your every curve. **YASMINA BOUHEBBEL**, from France, is teaching the dance to Irish women who find it gives them greater acceptance of their natural shape:

"It's a sensual, powerful way of expressing yourself. The moves are very centering because they concentrate around the hips and torso and head. The eyes are important too. It doesn't go against gravity, it works with it and so you feel very grounded when you practise it. You can be solid and graceful at the same time.

"I feel very free within myself dancing. It is an exclusively female dance. Arabic women used to it to express themselves in sacred rites which did not involve men. The dance is older than the Pyramids.

"Women have used it to alleviate period and labour pains. I have known many women who used it for this purpose.

"Unlike other forms of dance it allows you to be your own shape, yourself. Women really come to love themselves through it. The bigger you are the better it is. It's a real confidence booster.

"Novices are really shy about it and they find their esteem grows as they gain expertise. It liberates them. One woman from Kerry had the dance in her blood from the very first lesson. In a few weeks she did everything perfectly. She still does not have the confidence to perform in front of other people.

"But I can see the dance will do that for her eventually. That is its gift. It is a gift Irish women need because they tend not to feel as comfortable about their bodies.

"A woman's beauty is all about expression. When she learns to express herself there is nothing more beautiful."

Body meditation

JUDITH gets women to meditate on various parts of their bodies, to build up a familiarity with them. Try this exercise the next time you feel down about your looks/weight/bunions:

"Sit in a comfortable position, or lie on the floor. Take a deep breath, close your eyes and relax.

"Keep taking deep breaths until you reach a state where you are listening to your breathing. Then start to meditate on the various parts of your body you are trying to get in touch with. Go through the body, go through your feet, legs, buttocks, hips, the genitals , tummy, breasts, back, shoulders, arms hands, neck, throat, face and head. Try to include each part of your body.

"See how you feel about it. Look at any thoughts, feelings, images or attitudes related to that part of the body. For example around the sexual area, breasts and genitals, people often have attitudes about particular areas of their body that are almost like conditioned reflexes.

"Think about what has been said to you about them. If it is negative commentary recognise it as other people's comments — not yours. Tell that part of yourself you love it, because it is part of you. Talk to it about the hurt it has experienced. Let it know you will protect it in future.

"After you have done the exercise a few times let it know you like it. Tell it: 'You are part of me. Thank you for working with me. Thank you for functioning.' If you are in pain with that part, physically or mentally, let it know you will help it by loving it."

Body affirmation

ROSEMARY gives this exercise to clients. It's based on affirmation and response. Affirmation is a positive thought form to be presented into the subconscious. It's no use throwing it on top of a negative thought form. So what you do is you write down how much you love your body and how much pleasure it gives you and other people, then write down your response to that:

AFFIRMATION	RESPONSE
I, ... am beautiful the way I am	Yeah, right.
I have wonderful qualities	So why do I have such bad breasts/nose/legs
My partner loves my body	Why have all his other girlfriends been short/buxom brunettes?
I love my body	In the dark, under 10 layers of clothing.

Finish off with this affirmation:

"I, ... now know that I am a beautiful, loveable woman and that I deserve to be loved."

Look at the responses and see how many of them are actually true. Not many. It will become apparent to you just how many of your hang-ups are based on reality. If you do this exercise a few times then you will learn to deal with your responses and feel the effect of their negativity on you. Hopefully you will come to terms with them and kiss them goodbye.

Further reading
The Beauty Myth
by Naomi Wolf
Chatto and Windus
Real Gorgeous
by Kaz Cooke
Bloomsbury
Our Bodies Ourselves
by Jill Rakusen and Angela Phillips
Penguin

Chapter Nine

~ ~ ~ ~

MIRROR MIRROR...

"Mirror, mirror on the wall — who is the fairest one of all?"

THE WICKED STEPMOTHER asks her image to reaffirm the fact that she is beautiful on a daily basis. When it reveals her stepdaughter, Snow White, has taken her crown in the looks department she engineers a coup d'etat to get rid of her innocent, virginal relative. Who, in turn, answers a small advert in the personals:

"Wanted. Beautiful, helpless ex-princess to skivvy for seven men while waiting for her handsome prince."

Whether your favourite was Cinderella, Snow White or Sleeping Beauty, the fairy-tales we all grew up with establish one fact quite clearly: "Your face is your fortune'. So much emphasis has been placed on how we look that we can forget the sole purpose of fashion and beauty is to make us feel good.

No wonder certain feminists, for a time, felt they had to reject the hairdresser, beauty salon and fashion outlet in order to be taken seriously. They were dubbed 'ugly', and so people came to link the word 'ugly' with 'feminist'.

A fleet of female minds have analysed and written on this topic before, Betty Friedan, Germaine Greer, Naomi Wolf....

The frustration, isolation and anger experienced, where we all feel we need to have waspish waists, full breasts, slim hips and perfect facial features, have caused women a hell of a lot of grief over the centuries, let alone the present day.

Women worldwide through the ages have had to do terrible things in order to be fashionable and beautiful — stuffed into corsets, had feet bound, to name but two.

But we've also used fashion and beauty as a way of being ourselves. They are powerful forms of self-expression and when we use them to please us rather than others we get a tremendous amount of pleasure.

Dressing up and making-up is fun. That's what it's all about. Once we can learn to disregard the more controlling messages — the sexual sell used in advertising, the current trend of using painfully thin models which make anyone sensitive and over size-12 feel bloated and undesirable — and learn to dress and look the way that makes us feel good inside we are using fashion and beauty in a positive way.

The following pages contain insights from women who love fashion, love beauty treatments and yet don't feel under pressure to conform to a certain image or style. They get a tremendous sense of well-being and identity from how they choose to display and portray themselves.

Fashion conscious

RACHEL, 33 has a wardrobe full of fabulous clothes — all unique and eye-catching. She is elegant, graceful and stylish. You could describe her as fashion conscious. But she's not clad in minimalist gear and platforms. She's swathed in embroidery, brocade and rich, colourful fabrics. She has created her own fashion identity as she makes all her own clothes. She's even got her own Technicolour Dreamcoat:

"My favourite item of clothing has to be my coat, I've sewn on patches of material from every country I've visited — so I've sewn in memories in a sense and I carry them all around with me when I wear it.

"I've used clothes all my life to express myself — I even tried to make my school uniform look different. So I decided to make my own skirt — a wrap-around. I suppose my identity depended on it.

"Clothes help me to overcome my natural shyness. I don't have as much self-confidence as I appear to have — if I look more confident through my clothes then I feel more confident. Putting on something I made or that I choose to wear helps me to be myself — not what someone else wants me to be.

"I love layers — I find them really sensual and I love dance. So many cultures with strong dances have layered outfits, including our own. And I love colours — purples and dark reds. I notice them on other women too. They give me a sense of empowerment.

"I don't like man-made fabrics — they feel unnatural on my skin. My clothes are part of me so I like them to be as natural as possible.

"When I was a child my sister and I had a box of clothes for dressing up in. We had costume jewellery too. We were princesses.

"When I was in India travelling I was asked to model clothes. The Indian women don't like being photographed — they believe it takes their spirit away. They took us out into the desert and I found myself seated on a camel in a beautiful costume with tons of bracelets. It was my childhood princess fantasy come true.

"I think fashion is all about dressing up and being part of a fantasy. It enriches you, it's just for you and gives you a real sense of how wonderful it is to be a woman."

'Fat day go away'

EVA, 27: "When I was living in New York and having a 'Fat' day all I had to do was walk out on to the street to realise how much of it was just in my head. Outside there were all these Hispanic women with dead sexy outfits — crop tops and skirts in bright colours — looking really smiley because they believed they were gorgeous. They were mostly big women with real curves. They weren't ashamed of their shape. Their curves were there to be seen and flattered by what they wore — not hidden away."

Potions and lotions

HELEN, 25: "There is so much pressure on women to look good. There is a multi-million pound industry which rakes in money from women's insecurities. Selling them anti-ageing creams, stuff like that. I think they manage to do it because they have managed to persuade women that success is dependent on how beautiful they are.

" It has become too important to us. I think we are becoming more aware of this so things are changing, but too much emphasis has been placed on it, still.

"I love good clothes, I love to wear a little make up and mascara occasionally, but I do it for myself, not for anyone else, because it makes me feel good."

The 'feel good' factor

TRISH CAMERON, a sexuality tutor and trainer, feels dressing up and using make-up are wonderful ways of enhancing your sexuality and making you feel good.

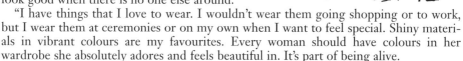

"A lot of the messages we receive can make us feel quite negative about ourselves. Some women can become afraid of dressing up because it gives them attention which might make them feel embarrassed . But it's simply dressing in a way that makes you feel good to enhance your sexuality. It's OK to hoover in your velvet dress if you're in the mood to look good when there is no one else around.

"I have things that I love to wear. I wouldn't wear them going shopping or to work, but I wear them at ceremonies or on my own when I want to feel special. Shiny materials in vibrant colours are my favourites. Every woman should have colours in her wardrobe she absolutely adores and feels beautiful in. It's part of being alive.

"I love putting on make-up — adorning my face and feeling beautiful. Enhancing your features is perfectly natural. But if you can't stir outside the door without a mask of make-up you aren't really confident in how you look without it. That can be symptomatic of low self-esteem. You have to feel good about yourself underneath the make-up. The make-up isn't you, it reflects you."

I look in the mirror, and what do I see?

GRAINNE, 31, is visually impaired. She has a deteriorating condition of the retina called RP. Just because she can't see what she is wearing doesn't mean she can't enjoy shopping or choosing clothes:

"I love natural fabrics. I go very much on the feel of things — cottons, silks, linens. My husband or sister comes with me when I am shopping to help me pick out the colours and styles I want.

"My sight has never been good, but now that I have lost an eye and have very poor sight in the other, I can only make out light and shadow. This doesn't mean colour doesn't affect my mood. I love reds and pale blues and when I have them on they really suit me and I can feel it.

"I wish sometimes I could judge in certain situations whether I am under- or over-dressed. I have to be reassured by whoever I am with. I rely on other people's descriptions to know what people look like or are wearing.

"I've arranged my wardrobe at home so I know exactly where everything is — I have all my dressy clothes to one side and my casuals to another and I remember what colour the clothes are, or I stick a safety pin to the label to help me remember: one for blue, two for red etc. I tend not to buy two of any item because you can get confused.

"I once bought two pairs of the same shoes in black and in red — it was really difficult to make sure they didn't get mixed up! I ended up sticking a plaster inside the black pair to help me remember.

"I don't tend to wear a lot of make-up but I do like it. I need to be reassured before I leave the house that my lipstick is not smeared or the colours don't clash with my clothes. But just because I cannot actually see it doesn't mean I don't like to enhance my appearance. I am a hairdresser's dream, because I tell them to do what they want, once they leave me with a fringe!

"Because we pick up 80% of our information visually, I tend not to feel so pressurised into looking a certain way or wearing a certain thing or being a certain size. I love being stylish, but I don't have to stare at the supermodels or slim women illustrating fashion in magazines. For me beautiful people have warm, friendly voices and firm handshakes. And fashion and make-up help me to express myself."

Which product? Which dress?

We're inundated with adverts for beauty products which, if you read the labels, insist they are the best because they contain everything from aloe vera to anti-ageing factors. How do you know which ones are best for you?

MORAG has years of experience in testing them as a magazine editor and loving sampler of things fashionable and beautiful:

"Different things suit different people and the price tag is not an indication of what is going to suit you. Cheap products can be as good as dear products, depending on your skin type. I've always encouraged women to find the product they like and then buy it. It might be a very expensive face cream, or a cheap one, but if it makes you feel better about yourself it's doing the job.

"I'd rather women feel they have a right to spend money on themselves, their bodies and the way they look rather than, and want to, feel they have to. Women are under a lot of pressure to work hard and rear families so in that sense we deserve to treat ourselves.

"Irish women don't treat or pamper themselves enough. I was talking to a couple of beauty therapists, based in rural areas, who find it difficult to find women, even in their own families, to try out new products for them. Many women don't like to even undo their top button!

"Making yourself up is almost seen as a form of showing off. That's a shame. There is a definite, genuine sense of style about Irish women but we don't pamper ourselves enough. Though we are coming around to it.

"The primary benefit of a good massage or facial is the treat element — the luxury of having someone look after you in that way is great for your self-worth. Booking yourself in for a beauty treatment is a lovely way of appreciating yourself. It makes you feel special because you're spending money on you and not on a new set of saucepans or the gas bill. It's not something you share with anyone else. It's a very personal statement of self-esteem. You don't necessarily look any better than you did when you went in, but you feel better.

"If you can identify what your pleasure is in life and give it to yourself now and then, you will feel better about yourself. Whether that pleasure is daily use of a skin cream or buying a good book and curling up to read it — you're entitled to it."

Fashion and the dreaded hipsters

With each passing year the trendiest gear seems to fit only the sylph like. Personally speaking, hipsters are my idea of a nightmare — the average pair wouldn't slide over my upper arm, let alone my upper thigh. How detrimental is it to the average Irish woman, the majority of whom would be around or over size 14/16, to see a host of new ranges for skinny ribs?

MORAG: "A woman needs to take personal responsibility for the way that she looks and dresses and the way she feels about her body, regardless of what society sees as fashionable. Admittedly it is hard to do that because we are bombarded by information and influences. But it's a myth that we have to tailor our bodies to what's available in the latest fashion. Clothes should be tailored to fit your body, not the other way around.

"Fashion is a fun thing to spend your disposable income on — it should not make you a slave or a victim. Women express their style in different ways.

"I've been immersed in fashion and fashion people for years, and I am now branching out in different directions of personal expression and career focus. It has been fun. I have worn things which, with hindsight, I am free to say looked awful on me. But I have never taken it seriously or seen it as the sole way to express myself.

"I love clothes and enjoy them but as I get older, and there is a sadness about this, there are things I can no longer wear because I feel foolish in them! At the same time I know women who don't feel like that and that is brilliant. I'd love to be a 60-year-old wearing lime green hipsters and crop tops and leather jackets.

"If you grow and develop as a person your style does change and become more individual and my sense of style has moved more into the way I think and speak. The clothes I choose to wear reflect that, rather than the clothes choosing me because they are this year's vogue.

Feeling good inside

Inner beauty is just as important as outer for enhancing your self-image and esteem. When we eat well and feel physically fit, life is a lot easier to cope with. We have been bombarded with diet and exercise regimes to the extent that we feel having a good diet and doing a proper workout is a very complicated occupation which needs a lot of analysing, calorie counting, scientific knowledge and stamina.

In fact the basics are so simple it's very easy to adapt a few principles into your life style at no significant extra cost to you: Here are some of them, taken from some free information leaflets provided by the Health Promotion Unit (for a full list of titles see Directory):

THE FOOD PYRAMID

The Pyramid helps you to plan your daily food choices, it is available in more detail in Health Promotion literature. Per day you need:
6+ SERVINGS of Cereals, Bread, Potatoes, Pasta, Rice
4+ SERVINGS of Fruit and Vegetables
3+ SERVINGS of Milk, Cheese and Yoghurt
2+ SERVINGS of Meat, Fish or Vegetarian Alternatives (Nuts, Pulses)
SPARINGLY: Fat and Oils, Confectionery and High Fat Snacks, Sugars, Alcohol.
(14 Units for women per week)

HEALTHY EATING TIPS

These are from the Health Promotion Unit's *Daily Healthy Choices* and *Be a Healthy Weight* leaflets. Here's a brief run-down on how to eat healthily and well:

Enjoy your food!
Eat a variety of foods from the Food Pyramid
Don't feel guilty after a slice of cheesecake
Eat the right amount of food
Exercise regularly
Don't eat too much fat — grilling, casseroling and baking are best
Each plenty of foods rich in fibre
Don't eat sugary foods with a high fat content too often
Don't eat too much salt — use herbs to flavour food instead
If you drink alcohol- keep within sensible limits
DRINK PLENTY OF WATER

EXERCISE

Let your body get some physical activity everyday.
Choose physical activity you enjoy rather then endurance tests.
Use exercise to get your whole body moving — such as walking, cycling, or swimming.

124

Warm up and cool down after exercise.

Exercise most days for at least 30 minutes.

Include exercise which strengthens muscles in your tummy and back.

STOP exercising if you feel unwell or dizzy or nauseous.

Consult your doctor before exercising if you have a health problem.

For weight loss, exercise at a moderate intensity for 30-60 minutes, is best for burning fat.

1. DRESSING UP BOX

Like Rachel's childhood fantasy fashion, it is really nice to be able to dress up, like you did as a child, when you swiped your mother's high heels, scribbled lipstick all over your face and thought you were a supermodel.

Get a box and go on a tour of the secondhand shops or sales. When you find things you love, but would never normally wear in real life — because they are too bright, too vivid, too dressy, too this, too that — buy them. Once you have the cash and they don't cost the earth. Put them into your dressing-up box. Jewellery, shoes, hats scarves... put them all in, why not?

When no one else is around or if you want to invite a few friends around who would find it fun — take out your dressing-up box, pull the curtains and dress up. You might get the courage to wear the treasures inside, out on the town some day.

2. BEAUTY JUST FOR YOU

It doesn't take much money or time to set aside two pampering hours a week — even if it's six in the morning, because you don't have any other time, this is worth getting out of bed early for.

A steaming hot shower or bath, a rub down with a small amount of aromatherapy oil mixed with rapeseed or olive oil, wrap your wet hair in a towel and spend a few minutes massaging yourself, using the palms of your hands in small circular motions. Slap some moisturiser on your face and smooth it in slowly, again with circular motions from the nose outwards. Do the same to your neck using upward strokes towards your jaw-line. Apply make-up if you wish.

Take the towel off your head and run your fingers over your scalp to revitalise it and then comb through your hair.

It's a simple, cost-effective routine and you'll feelrefreshed and revitalised afterwards.

3. CLOTHES SWAPPING SESSIONS

Call your friends and ask them to go through their wardrobes picking out things they are going to get rid of. Get together and swap some evening. One woman's cast off is another woman's desire.

4. NEXT-TO-NOTHING BEAUTY

SHARON CROWLEY runs an organisation called WOMEN UNLIMITED, apart from her stress management and personal development work she also runs courses in Quality of Living for those of us who haven't got a fortune to spend on ourselves.

Her beauty tips are based on products which don't cost the earth and you might find in your cupboard or fridge.

HAIR — many salons have a hairdressing school attached to them where you can have a cut, perm, highlights or re-style for a fraction of the salon price. All the students will be supervised so your hair won't be destroyed.

SKINCARE — Sharon warms up a small amount of olive oil to rub into her skin and mashes bananas for face-packs. If her eyes are tired she refreshes them by applying used tea-bags or slices of cucumber for a few minutes.

MASSAGE — Self-massage is a nice way to unwind, aromatherapy oils all differ in price, buy one that suits your pocket, mix a few drops with almond, grapeseed or olive oil and rub into your neck and shoulders

FACIAL STEAM — A pudding bowl of hot water, a towel and a few drops of aromatherapy oil and you have a facial steam to cleanse and open pores. Pull the towel over your head and lean over the bowl.

Further reading

Real Gorgeous
by Kaz Cooke
Bloomsbury

The Natural Beauty Book
by Anita Guyton
Thorsons

Chapter Ten

~~~~

ONE BANANA —
999 CALORIES

"My parents were trying to make me eat. I just couldn't. Then my step-dad put a banana in front of me with 999 calories written on it. We laughed at a time when there was very little laughter. I recovered." — *NIAMH*

THE FIRST WOMAN I EVER MET who suffered with anorexia told me that story — it never left me. She was a beautiful woman and I envied her serenity and her gorgeous, svelte figure. At the time I was dieting to try and lose a few extra pounds and she wanted me to know I was OK the way I was. It never occurred to me that being weight-obsessed could actually endanger your health.

There are many theories about eating disorders — bulimia and anorexia nervosa and compulsive overeating in particular. Books such as Fat is a Feminist Issue, by Susie Orbach and When Food becomes Your Enemy by Gillian Moore Groarke and Sylvia Thompson list any number of reasons for developing them, from using your excess weight to cushion you from the world to starving yourself as a form of subconscious protest at the world. And a plethora of explanations in between.

Whatever the reason, if you develop an eating disorder you have been made somehow to hate your body, to view it a prison, to see it as unacceptable to the world and yourself. What makes us feel so unacceptable?

Today anorexia, bulimia and compulsive over-eating have touched many lives. Most of us know someone who has a problem with food, a problem with the way they look. Nine times out of 10 that person will be female.

According to certain studies, 5 to 10% of young women become bulimic, 1 to 2% of adolescents and young women become anorexic. But most of us use food to comfort ourselves at some point.

Compulsive eating

How comfort eating develops into compulsive eating is something **ELAINE**, 30, can explain very well. She has just coming to terms it, thanks to a women's health course:

"I come from a family of big women. But I had no inclination that I was very fat, until someone asked me if my personal problems at that time had anything to do with my weight. I thought I was gorgeous. So, that was it, I started comfort eating then.

"I would eat any thing I could lay hands on, if I didn't have any money it would just be bread and butter. If I was flush it would be a Chinese, chocolates, biscuits... I didn't eat like that just because it was nice, I'd stuff myself, literally pushing down my feelings with the food. I had no restraint. I just felt I had to eat, even when I was sick from it. It went on for years and years. I could eat whole packets of biscuits and still want more.

"The realisation about what I was doing to myself came out of a women's health course. We discussed food and what a healthy diet was. I said to myself, 'I don't need all

that food — my body only needs a certain amount. I'm making myself feel better by having all this chocolate and biscuits, but they don't make me feel any better.' It was all in my thoughts.

"When the tutor started to talk about healthy eating she never once referred to my size or needing to diet. I didn't need to feel any more guilty about it. Weight never came into it, the principle was, whatever way you are, you can improve yourself, but you're also fine the way you are. Now, I'm at the point where I'm learning I am likable and as a matter of fact I'm wonderful. I don't always need food to reassure me. I don't need to hide behind my weight. Here I am world, love me, no matter what shape I bloody well am."

Anorexia

DONNA, became anorexic in her teens, she now runs self-help groups for those who suffer from eating disorders. She feels her need to be accepted by her family was what brought her to the point of starvation:

"I was very sensitive, I needed a lot of security and affection. In my family, those things just didn't happen. I hated my body from four years old. My mother wanted to change things about me. I started to diet because it was something she wanted me to do. Around the time my menstruation started my mother took me to a doctor for a diet because I was very chubby.

"I started comfort eating, then I started starving myself. I just yo-yoed between the two. By the time I was 17/18 I was about five-and-a-half stone. I collapsed.

"The sensation of food in my mouth was awful. Initially it is a voluntary choice, but then it is involuntary, you just can't go back. You can't find your way back to normality on your own. You have forgotten what normality is.

"When I lost weight I got a lot of attention. My mother would sigh a lot and tell me I was ruining her life. But it was still attention.

"Another thing was the messages I got to hide my body, my mother was always saying things like 'Cover yourself up!' I never got positive messages about being a woman.

"I was in hospital for quite some time. While I was there things were fine. I was given a 'big sister' who was further into recovery than I was. She would be with me when I ate.

"Even after coming out of hospital I felt that below my neck was an enemy that I could not control, a monster. I couldn't control my mind, a war was going on between my mind and my body.

"For a while the hunger screams at you and then it dissipates. At one point I would eat one chocolate biscuit a day and black coffee, avoiding vitamins, because that can trigger your appetite. At that time I loved looking at recipe books, walking around supermarkets and cooking for people and watching them eat. The more I starved the more I became obsessed with food.

"It was all to do with control. The only control I had in my life was food. I was powerless every other way.

"My recovery was slow and my reason for recovery was addressing the issues behind my anorexia. I learned that criticism of any kind is counterproductive, so the first thing I would say to sufferers is 'no more self-criticism'."

Bulimia

Bulimia might only have been named as a clinical condition in this century. But there are records of it which date back as far as the Roman Empire. The Romans would gorge themselves with food, make themselves sick, then eat again. It was a sign of wealth, the higher up the ladder you were, the more you gorged.

For **ROSEMARY**, 30s, it was a sign of self-hatred and despair:

"I was a single parent in New York with two children, one very sick. Bringing them up, alone, there I got to see how strong a person I was. Then I decided to come home to Ireland. I found that more stressful than everything I had gone through on my own. I had been away from home about 15 years, I felt I had no identity here, no function, after being away for so long.

"At the age of 25 I started to throw up. I felt totally out of control, using food for comfort. I ate and ate and ate. You actually get a 'high' from the gorging, even though you are bloated.

"When I was getting sick, I learned every crack and spot on the toilet bowl. You become so clever at being secretive about what you are doing.

"I would get terrible mood swings. The rage I had inside me, I never knew such anger.

"I launched myself straight into full bulimia, I didn't get sick on the odd occasion, it was every time I ate. Most bulimics have a 'grace period' between eating and getting to the toilet. In my mind I had six minutes before I started to digest what I had eaten. This lasted about two years before I realised what I was doing to myself and began to worry about the effect on my children. If I hadn't had them I don't know whether I would have been able to make myself stop.

"I hospitalised myself. The most beneficial thing about it was the space I got between myself and the world. I would have gone to jail — I just wanted out of the world of a while. During my recovery I read books, I gained knowledge and decided I wanted my life back. I never looked back except to tell other women of my experience to benefit them.

"When you have an eating disorder you feel completely alone, so it's good if former sufferers can participate in self-help groups, to convince the ones still going through it there is light at the end of the tunnel."

Hospital programmes

Some un-informed people would question why those with eating disorders need to be hospitalised for such long periods. But treatment focuses not just on eating again -it's about learning to live with yourself. An anonymous writer contributed this piece to the *Irish Times* last year, which explains how vital a long stay in hospital is for those chronically ill with an eating disorder. It is one of the most moving accounts of the anorexic experience. Unfortunately given its length it has been synopsised:

"I spent four months, 126 days, in St Patrick's hospital, Dublin, recovering from anorexia. Being covered by health insurance for this was vital not only for my present health but for my life.. My experiences were intrinsic to the formation of the basically happy, normal person...I am today. For the three years preceding it I literally missed 'life' existing in the prison that is anorexia nervosa. I felt myself to be trapped, totally power-less, alone...

"...I won't describe the history of my illness, suffice to say it began with an apparently faddish teenage diet....I am an absolute perfectionist...in a life where I seemed to exert no control over events that were critical to my world, I was creating a world where my control was complete...

"The more I withdrew from 'normal' life, the more I derived my only comfort from further emaciation, the more secretive, manipulative and ingrained my behaviour became... I hated looking like a Belsen victim but was terrified of losing the sense of sanc-tuary which only the behaviour and emaciation seemed to provide... I was terrified because I knew it was stronger than me.

"My decision to admit myself to the eating-disorder programme in St Patrick's was the most important I have ever made. With a huge sense of relief and final mental peace I relinquished all responsibility for my physical and mental care to the staff...

"At [first] the priority is to nourish the body sufficiently to make one receptive to mental therapy. But it is not a food-centred programme. A target weight is set but, more radically, a complete invasion of the individual's attitude to her world is sought to, quite literally, 'kill' the anorexic self and facilitate the re-emergence of the true person.

"...The programme is crucial because it recognises this subtle and essential point — the sufferer's inability to confront the deeper things going on in her world. ..The path to success is uphill, painful and long. Through the four months I gradually regained my relinquished independence...

"I did become quite attached to the hospital and the other girls on the programme. In a way they became almost a substitute for the anorexia. The gradual ejection from the nest — the progressive leave [weekend or day home visits] — was vital. Home visits were stressful at first as both my family and myself learned how to relate to each other without the anorexia factor.

"I don't know whether you can 'cure' anorexia... I gained, however, an awareness and an insight which has equipped me to suppress and control those traits... I existed in a nightmare..."

A nightmare faced only with and through the help of an eating disorder programme. Dr Elizabeth Cryan, who treats patients with eating disorders in a Dublin general hospital, has conducted a study into eating disorders:

"What it, and other similar studies revealed, is that eating disorders, anorexia and bulimia in particular, usually affect young woman. Patients with anorexia are often high achievers. Whatever the eating disorder, it really plays havoc in their lives.

"Patients with anorexia are much more likely to end up in hospital because their weight reaches a dangerous level and maybe they are developing fits of fainting or their blood count is starting to disimprove.

"On admission to hospital we would set a target weight and the patient would agree to it. We reassure them that we don't want to make them fat or pile weight onto them. We would look at a very small weight gain to start with, about a pound per week — anything more than that would be too fast.

"A nurse would sit with them throughout the meal, and for perhaps an hour afterwards, when their anxiety levels are at their highest. As they approach their target weight the controls around eating can be removed gradually to encourage the patient to see that they have the power of control themselves.

"Patients with bulimia would be encouraged to accept their current weight, agree to eat regular meals, keep a diary. This helps to create an awareness of what they are doing to themselves. Patients with bulimia can be admitted to hospital to build up the potassium levels in their body, but they are often treated as outpatients.

"About 50% of patients recover completely.

"A lot of the treatment depends on the patient themselves as they have to be very compliant. Also they have to cope with high levels of anxiety because by going on a feeding regime, they are exposing themselves to what they fear most. The fear of getting fat. They are putting that into someone else's hands which is very difficult to do. Unless people make a contract where they promise to eat and not to try to lose weight, it is difficult to make progress.

"There are lots of theories as to why people develop eating disorders. Also there seems to be an overlap between the two major clinical entities, anorexia nervosa and bulimia nervosa, in that many patients with anorexia nervosa go on to develop bulimia nervosa and many with bulimia nervosa go through phases of anorexia.

"One of the things that we did on the study was to ask the patients an open ended question: 'When I look in the mirror I see...?' The sort of words they used were very abusive: 'frumpy', 'disgusting'...

"Also people are very ashamed of their behaviour, they find it very difficult to eat with other people, you often find that they eat alone and they binge alone. They may have asked parents to lock the kitchen door and then they would forage and find the key, and they would feel very ashamed of this.

"Often the patients that we see will want to work in the food industry, they often describe cooking food for other people and then enjoying watching them eat it. Also they often have a great interest in dietetics — they tend to be expert calorie counters. In a sense they will be trying to have a very healthy diet too, or what they see as a healthy diet.

"I have had patients who chewed food and spat it out rather than actually swallow it and patients who gave themselves enemas, have taken laxatives and diuretics. There are different ways of purging. Then there is the exercise factor, often patients with anorexia will exercise compulsively — three to four hours a day in some cases.

"There is a sense of success in dieting, if you are failing in some aspects of your life or you have a sense of not having control, the experience of restricting your calorie intake may seem to alleviate those feelings. There can often be a sense of well-being and control from that success.

"Some people are restricters, they don't have any purging behaviours. They restrict their calories very effectively and lose a lot of weight, still feel fat and still aim to lose more. Other people will be of normal weight but will binge, starve themselves and then binge again.

"One of the things we ask people to do is to keep a diary each time they binge and write down how they felt about it. With some patients the binge might have been planned. They might have a bad day and find themselves saying 'When I get home I am going to eat and eat...'

"At the later stages of anorexia patients may lose their appetite, whereas early on your appetite is still there, but it is resisted because of the fear of getting fat.

"Many people with eating disorders are suffering from depression. Culturally there is a lot more pressure on women to conform to standards of slimness. Some patients with eating disorders have professions where appearance is very important — ballet dancers, models. Patients with anorexia tend to be achievement driven, perfectionists, though that does not hold across the board.

"Patients with bulimia tend not to have such a tendency to perfection. We find that a small percentage of patients with bulimia will tend to drink and engage in deliberate self harm, which they see as another way of relieving stress. It is much more common in patients with bulimia than in patients with anorexia nervosa, and in particular with patients that have been sexually or physically abused during childhood."

Living with a person who has anorexia or bulimia is a very stressful. Relatives have been known to go to great lengths to cook favourite foods only to find the sufferer does not touch a morsel. Many sufferers withdraw into their own world, and cut off those close to them. Watching someone fade away before your eyes, someone you care for, can be soul destroying. Many professionals treating eating disorders would ask the patient's relatives to come forward for family therapy.

Whatever your experience, as someone suffering from an eating disorder or as a relative, it is vital that you seek expert advice. All of the women I spoke to are well aware of the problems they have around food and themselves. They are compassionate women with extraordinary qualities, not least because of what they have been through. They are doing their best to come to terms with a world that demands so much from women, not just in terms of their appearance. It is little wonder that some sufferers have perfectionist tendencies — since we are so often expected to be perfect. There seems so little room to be human and have flaws, but being human is all we can really be.

Dr Cryan's work, the work of the self-help groups and the other eating disorders centres around the country, puts a large amount of emphasis into giving you the courage to accept yourself, to have faith in your capabilities and understanding of your insecurities. To be you.

Further reading
Fat is a Feminist Issue
by Susie Orbach
Hamlyn

Real Gorgeous
by Kaz Cooke
Bloomsbury

The Anorexic Experience
by Marilyn Lawrence
Women's Press

When Food Becomes Your Enemy
by Gillian Moore Groarke and Sylvia Thompson
Mercier Press

Chapter Eleven

~~~~

ROAR!

Pregnancy and Motherhood

"I loved the final part of giving birth — the pushing. Loved it. Each time you roar 'Yes. Yes.'"
— JENNIFER, 27

THIS CHAPTER LOOKS AT THE emotional changes of pregnancy and childbirth — getting in touch with yourself and your baby — thinking about your baby. Holding the baby in your emotions, putting your hand on your stomach when it kicks, feeling the position it is lying in, spending time alone with soft music and your bump, thinking about what it will be like when it arrives, is a wonderful way of waiting for a new arrival.

> **JENNIFER**, 27: "When I laughed, then I'd get this fantastic, warm feeling in my stomach! I really did. That was the highlight of the pregnancy — through laughter, I felt him there. That I was building up a relationship with him."

> **MICHELLE**, 30s: "It's the shortest and longest nine months of your life"

We need to take time out to get in touch with ourselves when we're carrying a new life. It's important that we make decisions about the birth, the future, ourselves. It's important we can face childbirth and motherhood without fear and with realistic expectations of what it will involve.

MARGOT McCAMBRIDGE has nurtured thousands of newborn babies and 'newborn' mothers through the process of bonding, feeding, caring and learning about their child, and themselves. She is a wonderful, wise woman — every new mother should have someone like her to help her through pregnancy and childbirth.

She takes the biggest fears of the mother or what she calls 'can be mothers' on board and gives them what they need — encouragement.

MARGOT is counsellor/therapist and also works part-time as a public health nurse (registered nurse and midwife with diploma in public health) visiting new arrivals and new mothers in their home. She is speaking here as a private individual who treats women having trouble adjusting to the motherhood role:

"I care about mothers and babies. When I worked as a health visitor in the UK I was required by statute to visit them at least once in their home, but often I would go back three or four times if I had the time — because I loved it. Mothers and babies are part of the biggest joy and miracle life has to offer.

"Each pregnancy is different, each child is different, each labour is different, each mother is different. It's a unique and individual experience.

"I've learned that there are NO rules and regulations, when it comes to mothers and babies. Because hospitals, by necessity, have to be governed by rules, we have to be careful a mother's needs are not missed.

"The other thing that I think women are not prepared for, is the first six weeks after the baby is born. There is, what we call in analytic terms, 'a folie a deux', between mother and baby. It's a dance.

"The baby, initially, doesn't know that it's separate from its mother. It's been in the mother's tummy and the contact is still close. The baby knows the mother by smell, knows the mother by touch, knows the mother by the sound of her heart-beat; it's a very intimate knowing, because s/he's been inside the mother's tummy.

"The baby needs mother to interpret his or her needs. So it can be really difficult for a mother to adjust to that. When the baby cries, do you know if it's a hungry cry, if it's a nappy cry, if it's a windy cry? There's a huge amount of learning to be done."

JENNIFER, 27, has just gone through her six-week *folie a deux* — LUKE was eight weeks at the time of interview:

"Coming home, which should be fantastic, wasn't for me. It's nothing to do with 'I don't like this baby.' You just can't stop crying. Anything — happy or sad — would make me cry.

"I suppose that you just feel like, it's all your responsibility. It's a strange time. You just don't feel like you, anymore. You don't feel like the person you were five days ago. You're nothing like that person. I now am again, but it took this long.

"I couldn't read anything that wasn't about babies for the first two weeks. I didn't listen to the news. I didn't care about anything. It was a gradual thing, coming back into the world, as an individual, as an adult. I feel that as you get to know the baby better, you get to know yourself, as a mother, better. You're learning too. The baby trusts you so much, that you do get this feeling of — 'I am capable.'

"The baby causes the Confidence Crisis, to begin with, but then it's the baby that builds the confidence back up. I feel happier than I ever did."

MARGOT: "The only thing most mothers depend on, is the one experience we all have as mothers/can-be mothers — we were all babies. So, at some very deep level, we know what our own mothering was like.

"Apart from the mother's knowledge we, as professionals, also know more about pregnancy, childbirth and baby nurturing than ever before.

"We now know, through ultrasound studies, that babies behave the same way after they're born, as they did in the womb. The mother should be able to tell you how the baby is doing rather than you always telling her. If that does not happen that is taking some of her power away.

"If you listen to the language of childbirth professionals they say things like: 'I delivered the baby....' They didn't — the mother did. It isn't the doctor or midwife who deliver, they assist, mothers deliver."

The experience of birth

When women have not had children the first thing they want to know is what it feels like. Here are some accounts from mothers who've had home births, Caesareans, hospital births and waterbirths:

JENNIFER, 27: "The morning of the day our baby was born, when the contractions started, Joe looked up what to do next in a book. The heading: 'Things To Do Now' said things like: 'Relax. Phone a friend. Make a casserole'. Joe said — 'You'd better wait, I'm going to get the ingredients for the casserole!'

"Later, in the hospital, I was surprised at how difficult I found it to cope with the pain. I thought that I'd be able to reason with myself, that it would be over very soon. You do hit the point of despair, when you're not even close to the pushing stage.

"The epidural made an enormous difference. The only thing is that you have to stay still for it. It's really difficult, when the contractions are coming on top of each other. You've no break... But I was very glad it was available.

"I was very conscious of not being abusive. I think it's a really stupid thing, to start shouting accusations at your husband and the midwife. I was terrified in that hour, between getting the epidural, and actually giving birth. I had this feeling of doom. It was the terror of something being wrong.

"Up to that you're too busy. But that last hour was very, very quiet, and there was just a midwife sitting beside me, waiting for me. The hospital staff were gorgeous — really kind, they reassured me at every turn about what was happening.

"Then, they said — 'Alright. Let's go!' That was a bit exciting. I could take an active role again, I could do something, not just be the victim. I loved that part of it — the whole pushing. Loved it. Each time you roar "Yes. Yes."

"Then his head came out and they were saying, 'Look at the head.' I couldn't look at it over my stomach. I couldn't see. Very soon after, the little body came out, and there he was.

"Incredible. I thought I would cry. I was just laughing. I was really, really happy. I wasn't emotionally drained. I was really invigorated. I felt great. I felt brilliant. I felt that he was there and that was all that mattered."

RACHEL, 30s: "When I found I was pregnant it was very much wanted and half-planned! I didn't want to go to hospital because I'm not that keen on them, though I know Irish nurses and midwives are fantastic. I read a lot in making my decision to have a home birth.

"I decided to have a birthing pool so I could get in when pain escalated and ease my back. The labour was long but it wasn't constant and I did things like go for walks and slept, played Trivial Pursuit. To be honest it was a bit boring! Every time I was measured I had only dilated by half-a-centimetre — that was disheartening. The baby wasn't in any distress at all, the midwife checked her heartbeat regularly. I met the midwife 12 weeks into the pregnancy so I was sure of her.

"Because my partner was concerned I decided to have another friend with me so it would take the pressure off him. That was great, we needed three people as it took so long! For me the pain relief was the support they gave me.

"When she came into the world everyone burst into tears. The emotion was that of achievement. It was the most beautiful feeling. She was 10 and half pounds! It was really lovely and gentle in the water and I am convinced it was the right birth for her — she was so relaxed."

JOANNE, 39: "Some women might think I'm crazy but I actually enjoyed the birth. The hospital staff answered all my questions and made me feel part of their team. Yes, there is pain but when you know what is at the end of it is worth it.'"

MARY, 30s: "One thing you really need is patience when you are in labour! But you do have funny moments. I had this lovely fireman who was in doing his training when I was having my first baby. He walked up and down with me chatting away and ended up asking one of the nurses out!

"I didn't feel embarrassed by his presence at all. I remember a friend of mine telling me years ago that if Robert Redford walked in while you were in the delivery room you wouldn't give a curse. Being embarrassed goes out the window when the contractions are coming thick and fast. If they said a handstand would help, you would do that to the best of your ability to get the baby to come out.

"I've had four children and I have to say the difference in the hospital treatment is phenomenal. When I went in to have to Steven years ago I had an enema, then they shaved you. There's very little of that business now. When you go into hospital make sure that you can say the words 'No' and 'Why?' Audrey was very big but because I felt more in control it was the best labour I had, it was like being in a hotel compared to the others."

ELAINE 30: "On my first I was 22 and I was petrified. My blood pressure was sky high, I was ready to have a stroke. The baby's life was in danger, in the end they did a section.

"The staff in the hospital were brilliant, I got to know them all, I was in there many times, before the birth. I really felt like I was in good hands and, although she was in danger they kept saying everything would be fine. I put all my trust in them. She was in an incubator and when I went to see her, the feeling just comes from your toes, it is over-whelming.

"On my second I was more in control, which is what you need. You cease to be in control, if you don't ask exactly what is happening every step of the way. I do think it's not natural to lie down — you should be standing or kneeling and let gravity take its course."

MICHELLE, 30s: "After a Caesarean learning to walk properly again is the hardest thing. You think you are running and then some granny on a zimmer frame passes by. It takes a long time to stand up straight again! You pass clots for a couple of weeks after having the baby. Ask for as much information as you can before you leave the hospital, if you've had a section. I was given all the information I needed to make sure I knew how long the recovery would take. The care in the hospital helped a lot and it was nice to have a rest before returning home.

"Having a Caesarean is hard but having the baby in your arms makes it all worth it."

Problems with the new arrival

"The more she cried the more nervous I became, the more nervous I became the more she cried. It was very harrowing and I felt like throwing her out the window sometimes. I couldn't admit it to anyone — imagine not liking your own baby." — SARAH, 34

What do you do if your little bundle of joy turns into a little bundle of screams?

MARGOT: "The conditioning which we are brought up with is 'Babies are lovely, so we always love them. We never get angry, there's no room for the angry feelings'. There is no room for the feeling, 'I don't want to know about this baby. This baby's frustrating me to death.'

"It's alright to feel like that — it's not alright to act out the anger or frustration on the baby, but it's OK to feel like that. Even if a baby is behaving well it will still disturb the routine you had established for yourself before motherhood. We are not told enough about that. And taking care of another human being is also an all-consuming task.

"Looking at feelings — for me that is the thing that needs to be addressed in the whole business of pregnancy, delivery and post-natal care.

"I have seen mothers who can run a business, no problem. They have a baby — they just go to bits; because it's nothing to do with your head, it's nothing to do with what the books tell you, it's nothing to do with what the doctors and nurses tell you.

"What it has to do with is: — 'I wake up in the morning and I feel I can't cope. I feel awful and tired. I want to sleep. I'm up all night. This baby is always at me. It's demanding. What am I going to do?'

"It's suddenly a situation where, instead of running your life like a business, as you did before, you have to respond to a baby — not control the baby. We're not geared to responding at all.

"That's where the shock comes in. I learned this a long time ago. I was working as a student nurse in a Paediatric Unit — a baby unit — and I was feeding 15 babies, three times a night. It was no bother at all. Then one of my relatives asked me to mind her baby daughter for a day. 15 babies a night — no bother. Just one baby didn't seem a problem.

"I thought the mother would never come home that night.

"There's a personal involvement — even though it wasn't my own baby, she's my relative. It wasn't just a question of feeding her, I had to look after her in every way. In a hospital, someone else takes over on the next shift — you're not with them 24 hours, it's a job.

"That was only one day that I experienced. Can you imagine, when you're totally unprepared for this motherhood role, and you have it all day, every day?

"Animals do it naturally and humans can do it — depending on their own mothering. But animals are not as interfered with, in society, as mothers are. They're not controlled. Society says, 'This is how you do it.' And mothers are expected to follow."

Home births

MARGOT: "If you're having a baby at home, you can be discouraged from it. But the home midwives give a great service, they're on call and give 10 days postnatal care. I've had some experience of home deliveries and they were super because it's a very normal environment, everyone in the family is involved.

"If the mother is at home she is in control but when you're in a hospital it is very hard to be that assertive. So much depends on the midwife. If the midwife really listens to you, you're fine. You have to be flexible, if you're planning a home birth and there are medical complications you have to be prepared to go into hospital if anything is amiss or wrong. If someone has a premature baby it is difficult for them too because they are not prepared for an early delivery."

Home birth midwives will refer mothers to hospital if they go into labour before 36 weeks or if there are complications.

GILLIAN DUNLOP is co-ordinator of the Home Birth Centre of Ireland:

"I think pregnancy is not just about childbirth. It's about the wider and the broader issue of what it means to be a woman. Deciding how to have your baby should also take into account the kind of person you are.

"I don't think women have to have home births. They should be given the information to make a decision about whether to have one. If they choose not to have a baby at home women should at least have more flexibility in hospital births.

"Birthplans, where you decide with your doctor and midwife what way you want to have your baby, are important. It would also be more reassuring to have one person looking after you, instead of a lot of different people throughout your pregnancy. It is meant to be a private, intimate moment and you need to build up a trust with the professionals.

"Nowadays women have fewer babies and better sanitation, nutrition and antenatal care, there's no statistic to say hospital is better than home. But people are led to believe it is. They think it's illegal or something their grannies did. It wasn't so long ago that lots of babies were born at home.

"The domiciliary (home-birth) midwives would say if the mother is calm, relaxed and in control of getting on with labour, without interference, her body will perform the way it is meant to, the baby will not be distressed. In the majority of cases that is how it turns out.

"I'm not saying there are no women who need hospital intervention, but we need to look at how necessary the intervention is and the snowball effect it can have. There is a lot to be said about being assertive no matter what road you take -home or hospital.

"A lot of women find out their rights when they decide to have a home birth by word of mouth, or through Cuidiu — Irish Childbirth Trust, or the Home Birth Centre of Ireland. They can find out about financial rights, finding a midwife, meetings with other parents. I don't offer my own two wonderful experiences unless asked. I try to be more objective.

"Having decided to have a home birth your financial rights depend on the health board area you live in. Most pay a maximum of £400, or two thirds of the cost, some pay only £250. Midwife fees are normally £700 to £800. You have to make up the shortfall. VHI consider every application in its own right. If you're on social welfare you could try applying to your health board for a more substantial grant.

"*Women in Ireland, Knowledge, Attitudes and Behaviour to Health Care*, an ERSI Book, said that of the women they surveyed, 5% had home births. And of the women who didn't have home births 14% expressed an interest in having one."

ANNIE, 25, has had experience of hospital and home births. She describes her first birth at home:

"I went into labour in the early morning and had a beautiful day staying in touch with my baby and my partner. Friends called around — it was so relaxed. We popped out in the evening to get bananas and it really started to happen! I kept rotating my hips on the walk home — my partner was very embarrassed!

"A few hours later and I was ready to deliver, it was very intense. The midwife was wonderful 'You're almost there — you're doing fine.' She said all the things I wanted to hear.

"I wanted to push but had to hold back, the only way I could bear to be was on my hands and knees, the floor was covered in plastic sheeting and I had a bean bag under me to support me. The baby just came out! It was amazing, the midwife was so excited, she left me in peace with him and made me a cup of tea. The first cup of tea after birth is the nicest you'll ever have. For the next three weeks we slept in that room, on the mattress, just being together. Beautiful.

"On my second baby I was diagnosed with diabetes 10 days before the baby was born. The midwife took me to hospital straight away. I was terrified of needles and I had to have four injections a day.

"It was so impersonal compared to being at home. I cried a lot. I found the pain much more unbearable, because with the diabetes I had to have drugs and I had to give birth on my back.

"My baby was over 11 pounds when she was born. It took me a long time to recover. I know a lot of that was down to my own fears and the fact I went into hospital with a serious condition, but when you've given birth at home there is no other method to match it in my opinion."

Breast-feeding

MARGOT: "If the mother produces a live, healthy baby, everyone is pleased but if she has had a painful delivery the mum mightn't be ecstatic about greeting the new arrival. If she is exhausted and in pain it may be very difficult for her to put this child to her breast. These moments are so important and this needs to be recognised and responded to appropriately."

We know that breast is best for your baby, both in terms of closer contact and in terms of building up the baby's immune system. The instructions are simple: lift the child, put it to your breast, let it suck, milk comes out. Again, MARGOT comes back to the feelings being more daunting than the actual physical process:

"It can be very daunting to take on board all the new things you have to learn once your child is born — breast-feeding is the most natural thing but it can very hard for a nervous mother.

"I met a woman once who had just given birth to a beautiful bab. She was wearing a nipple shield because she was so sore with failed attempts to feed. I helped her to put the baby on the breast, and the baby started to suck immediately. 'It's so easy!' the mother said. 'This is great!'

"'Why wouldn't it be?' I asked her. It turned out she had received feeding instructions in the middle of the night in hospital when she was exhausted. 'I just wanted to sleep' she said to me.

"We need to let the mother decide what is best for her and her baby. We can only support her as professionals. Her needs are the ones that must be met .

"People and professional people tend to forget childbirth is all to do with feeling and little to do with mechanics."

JEAN, 40s, bottle-fed her first two children, then breast-fed her third:

"I was very young and I had nobody to tell me how to breast feed. I thought my first baby, Sally, was hungry because she was crying. I just gave her a bottle and found I had a much happier baby. If I had relaxed in the first place she could have been fine.

"Breast-feeding is about being being at ease, replenishing your stocks, basically. I was running around and she would sense the tension in my body. Older relatives weren't supportive — if you breast-fed, it was an admission of poverty. One would send me upstairs to a cold room to feed the baby rather than in comfort surrounded by family. I see people feed babies by breast much more easily now.

"When I had Cliona my breasts were very sore after she was born, and I fed her for maybe two or three weeks, just to give her a start. But it wasn't right. Sally was two and needed attention and, again, it was easier to bottle feed.

"Then Maeve came along, I was that bit older, more relaxed and less obsessive. I started to lie in bed to feed her. I just let her nuzzle away as long as she wanted and then switch over. I breast-fed her until she was 16 months, and she gave me up rather than the other way around. I took her into bed one morning and she just spat me out and said 'Nah, don't like it'."

Coming home

MARGOT: "I think that men have a hard time, because they are not really able to empathise with pain, childbirth and stitches, sore nipples and mother's intuition. They can sympathise but not empathise. If a baby awakes at night the mother will be awake immediately but the dad might sleep right through it, because psychologically women have a deep intuition which I call 'Women's Knowing', you won't find it in any text book but it is there."

WHAT IF I'M NOT DOING IT RIGHT?

"I've got a a Masters degree, and am studying for a PhD. But taking care of an eight-pound one-day-old felt like the most insurmountable task. It got easier once I stopped confusing myself with all the theories and learned to trust myself — and the baby." — **DEIRDRE**, 42.

MARGOT: "New mothers are vulnerable. You feel your baby is so delicate you are afraid of hurting it. Of course it is in one way, but it's also very resilient. Mothers feel the huge burden of responsibility. Whatever you need to do to make your child comfortable and happy, and you comfortable and happy, is OK.

"There are no set patterns or rules and if you don't follow the child-rearing books to the letter you're not a bad mother. Ignore the messages which say 'That's not the right way, this is the right way...'

"You're not supposed to be terrified, but you might be. You're supposed to think all babies are lovely — but they mightn't be. One woman came to see me and she said 'I don't know, he keeps crying, I can't stop him, what am I supposed to do?' My first job was to reassure her it was OK to feel frustrated.

"Instinctively you will have a sense of what to do and what is comfortable, that just needs to be encouraged. I say to mothers 'trust what feels right for you' and they look at me in amazement.

"We spend most of our lives ignoring our instincts, but pregnancy and childbirth is the one time when you really need to trust them. You should trust your instincts at all times in your life but particularly then. The emotions are open because they need to be open for you to understand how your baby is feeling.

"I try to help midwives as well as mothers, to tune into the mother. I do think midwifery is women's business — I make no apologies for that. Women can be much more in tune with what a delivering woman is going through — I don't think it's as simple as saying it's because they are female. But I think you have a better chance of a woman understanding the process than a man. Down through the centuries it has always been women responsible for helping mothers give birth.

"Just after childbirth, in the next six weeks, you have what is known as the wet period. The milk is flowing, the blood is flowing, the tears are flowing. Every mother will cry during the first six weeks, sometimes tears of joy, sometimes sadness, sometimes frustration, but there will be tears. This is normal.

"When the tears flow for longer than six weeks, or the mother feels really down, you find you may have postnatal depression."

Mother taught me everything I know

"The depression will be an expression of past experiences too. It will be a time when you remember your own mother and how she looked after you.

"If a woman has not had a good experience of her own mother she will often try to do the exact opposite with her own child and what you have there is the flip side of the same coin, which can be just as difficult."

For instance if your mother never hugged you, you might smother your own baby with affection. If your mother never gave you things, you might spoil your own child. If your mother was forbidding you might end up never saying 'no' to your own child.

However it can be a positive experience too. Older women who have reared families can give the time and energy over-stretched Public Health nurses can't. So calling on your aunt, granny, mammy's experience can be helpful.

MARGOT: "If you have a close family there is tremendous family support and that is what you need. I've seen older women give so generously of their time and really guide young mothers through the first few stages. That's what family networks are all about — supporting each other."

It's positive — I'm pregnant!

JENNIFER, 27: "We were due to get married in May 1996, in Sorrento, Italy. We came back, from the two week expedition to sort out the wedding, to discover that I was pregnant!

"I thought it might be gall-stones, I was feeling a little bit funny. I took a pregnancy test to eliminate that from the equation. Of course I'm not pregnant — I couldn't be. I was!

"We didn't speak for about five minutes, then we were thrilled. Our first thought was — isn't it brilliant, we can have kids!"

"Experts say about half of all pregnancies are unplanned. After the initial shock, you begin to prepare for the new arrival, but most people take a lot longer than five minutes!

MARGOT: *"There is a significant difference between an unplanned and an unwanted pregnancy. It takes a lot longer to adjust to an unwanted pregnancy. But the thing is you have nine months to adjust, almost a year, a considerable amount of time."*

As your body changes so your emotions change, if you allow them.

MARGOT: "I have a very simple view on this — your body knows what is best for you. For instance when I got pregnant I really did not want a child at that stage of my life. I was 41 and my partner and I had planned not to have babies. I miscarried. I believe I would make a much better mother now than I would have made then. I have a huge sadness about not having had a baby, but there is another part of me which recognises my mothering instinct is fulfilled looking after other mothers and babies. And I have step-children too. That's how it is for me.

"I know what it feels like for a pregnancy to take you by surprise — I freaked. You really do need to be clear in your own mind whether you want a child or not. Again people automatically assume it is great to be pregnant — I found that hard to deal with and I am sure other mothers do. Not everyone wants a child. Mothers-to-be can feel very guilty about not wanting the new life growing inside them.

"You can adjust. Women in the situation of a surprise pregnancy might need counselling or at least someone to talk to about it, once the counselling is non-directive i.e. not pushing a woman in a particular direction. You need someone who will listen."

When is the best time to have a baby?

MARGOT: "Bodywise between 19 and 28 is probably the best time. Women can bear in mind that if you are in the middle of a career, babies interrupt, whereas if you are younger your career is either babies or you are putting a career on hold or go slow until they are older.

"Now women are both career and baby-orientated, they should think quite seriously about their child plans, because many women find themselves overwrought with trying to handle both. That's not to say you can't be a good mother and go to work — I think how you plan it is extremely important. How are you going to give the necessary time to your baby and yourself?

"I know this might prove difficult for some women to understand, but I have seen mothers with phenomenal guilt complexes about going back to work. You need to work out what you're going to do beforehand, ideally, to reach an arrangement that will suit both you and the baby.

"You're making the choice also for your baby. You have to make sure they get the attention they need. A young baby needs individual attention i.e. from one mother figure. That doesn't have to come from its own mother full-time — but it is preferable to find a reliable child-minder who can be a constant in the young life and who will get to know the child's needs as well, or almost as well, as you do.

"It's very tough for a mother — to survive most women have to work. They also need stimulation outside the home. We need to make allowances for that in our society. Job-sharing is a good idea, because in my experience most women with children do want stimulation and some sort of job, but they do not want full-time work outside the home. When I was Director of Nursing in a hospital I offered as many job-sharing posts as possible.

"One of the reasons I wanted it that way was (a) I saw young nurses who just couldn't cope with the two work-loads and I felt sad about that and (b) when we brought in the job-sharing they loved being at home one week and they also loved coming to work the next week — so we actually got a better service.

"Women who job-share are often even more hardworking and conscientious than full-time employees. Society really should allow for more job-sharing — for men too so they can have be more involved in bringing up their children.

"In this country we talk about family values — but we do not support mothers and fathers in the way they need to be supported. The business fraternity dictate, by and large, the nature of society and there is no sympathy in this country for mothers and babies.

"The most important job in the world is bringing up children, creating and nurturing the next generation."

Miscarriage

Certain studies show almost 25% of known pregnancies will end in miscarriage and nearly one in four women will miscarry. The aftermath of a miscarriage can be very traumatic and many hospitals can help with this, putting couples in touch with counsellors if needed:

ELAINE, 30, and **PAUL**, lost a baby last Christmas. The hospital helped Elaine to come to terms with her miscarriage:

"I have a boy and girl and wanted one more child, so I was delighted when I got pregnant. But looking back, from day one, I had an instinct that I wasn't going to carry the baby. I looked after myself really well. But coming up to Christmas, I started bleeding and went to hospital. I was devastated. There was nothing they could do at that point as I had haemorrhaged badly. I cried and cried, I knew I was hurting and I had to let it go. The hospital was brilliant. Paul felt guilty for not helping me enough in general during the pregnancy, he couldn't accept that these things happen.

"Afterwards we went on a holiday with the family, the children helped me to get over it. I came home and found a letter from the hospital, rang them, and they said that they had the foetus.

"After Paul and I talked, we eventually decided to bury it with his grandmother and that was great — having something to grieve for. We also went to see it in the mortuary. It was so tiny — only three months old. Seeing it made a great difference, it made it all real.

"Not many people came to the service, but I didn't need many. We just wanted to say goodbye and let it know it was loved. I didn't realise how hard it was having a miscarriage until it happened to me. My sister in law was great because it happened to her twice, and she was able to understand how I felt.

"I can go to the little grave and feel for the baby I never had."

Birth without fear

Many women fear the pain of childbirth, **JUDITH** — who had her first child at home at 37 — decided she was not going to allow those fears to take her over:

"I had done years of things like relaxation, breathing, exercising. I just kept telling myself 'It's going to be easy, it's going to be fine'. I did it through surrendering to my body. It knows how to give birth instinctively, so I had to let my body take care of things.

"Now that's very hard for the head to take — there are all kinds of mental obstacles in the way. I had my first child at 37 — that's quite late and the odds against a nice labour were stacked against me. But I managed, through meditation and breathing, to have a two-hour labour, with no pain and the birth was absolutely fine. I'd also talked to the baby a lot in the last few stages of pregnancy, telling him his environment was going to change, the waters were going to break and by not panicking we would be helping each other.

"It is a huge shock to the system, however, to have a child later in life. I had never really been around a baby before so I really didn't know what I was letting myself in for. I had to stay up at night and breast-feed — it was just so difficult! I kept thinking I just had to get back to normal as soon as possible and there really isn't a 'normal' once you've had kids.

"The reality is when you're older you don't have the same amount of energy. I always say I have two personal fitness trainers — one called Daniel and one called Jack and they just keep you on the move.

"On the other hand, because I had my children late, I am not thinking 'They're tying me down — I hate them!' I've done so many of the things I wanted to do, I'm in touch with myself. Women often rush into having children without really thinking about the consequences or whether they are ready for them.

"I have a great sense of freedom with my kids. We have great fun together. My partner says: 'I have a six-year-old son Daniel and he is a great friend.' My children teach me things every single day. How to live for the moment, have fun, cry when you're upset, be angry, be happy."

What do I want to make of my life?

MARGOT believes women need to ask themselves this question in relation to having children:

MARGOT: "The pace of life can be inhuman, women can lose touch with themselves and in losing yourself you lose your most vital asset. Do you want to come home from work, exhausted and have no time with your child? And in the evening the child will be most demanding because they have not seen you all day.

"I believe it is very tough for women now, tougher than it was years ago because now they're expected to do two jobs. Before, they didn't have a choice about it, but at least they only had one job.

"Being you, being a mother, can raise difficult issues, so maybe we feel we have to keep going 24 hours a day so we don't have to look at them or ourselves. Everyone needs space, especially mothers because they are meeting anothers' needs so much.

"A lot of people turn up in therapy in times of crisis. Pregnancy can be a time of crisis — however well planned you are it rarely turns out as you expect it to.

"I think a lot of women need to be mothered — especially when they're pregnant or coping with a newborn infant."

Pregnancy — part of who you are

"I felt my first ghost when I was pregnant, because my feelings were so open. I feel so deeply what is going on when I am pregnant." — **SUZY**, 38

So we come back to the points made in the beginning, full circle. Pregnancy in a rushed world is hard to get in touch with. But it is important to put your foot down and find time for yourself and your baby, what's happening to you is one of the most momentous events of your life:

MARGOT: "I have talked to women in their 80s who remember their pregnancies in detail. You never forget them or childbirth. It is part of who you are.

"It is the deepest bond there is, apart from the one shared between partners. At a subconscious and conscious level we carry it always. Even those not related to us will relate to pregnant women in a deep way. I know one psychotherapist working with a child, through play, who was told by the child she was pregnant. She found out afterwards that she was three months gone!"

Recommended reading
THINKING ABOUT YOUR BABY
by Martha Harris

THE BOOK OF CHILD
Pregnancy to 4 Years Old
Health Promotion Unit

MISCARRIAGE
by Dr Martine Millett and Dr Ann Byrne-Lynch
A Health Promotion Unit booklet

EVERYWOMAN
by Derek Llewellyn-Jones
Penguin

THE EXPERIENCE OF CHILDBIRTH
by Sheila Kitzinger
Penguin

OUR BODIES OURSELVES
by Angela Phillips and Jill Rakusen
Penguin

BIRTHTIDES — Turning towards HOME BIRTH
by Marie O'Connor
Pandora

GREAT EXPECTATIONS: Having a Baby in Ireland
by Beverley L. Beech and Máire O'Regan
Mercier Press

Chapter Twelve

~~~~~

SAVAGE

"Whenever I am stressed out I call an all-party conference with my hormones. If they are not respected my body is not respected and I start to behave like a bit of a savage."
— SUZANNE, 28

HORMONES STIMULATE AND GOVERN every stage of our development. In that respect they get a lot of bad press. Many women put down problems caused by a pressurised lifestyle to hormone imbalance. The only solution is then to accept symptoms like fatigue, depression, irritation and crying bouts as facts of life, to be accepted and to be coped with as best we can.

Arabella Melville, in her book *Natural Hormonal Health* has this to say about hormones and a healthy lifestyle:

> "...Hormonal health means health for the whole woman; glowing health that gives you the energy you need to get the best out of every day, whatever the time of the month, whatever the time of your life. When your hormones are in balance, you will have access to all the strength, power and productivity that is a woman's birthright."

The key to good hormonal health lies in understanding your hormones and also in coming to terms with the rites of passage in every woman's life, signalled by hormonal and emotional change.

DR MARY SHORT, a GP with a special interest in women's medical issues, explains the hormonal changes a woman experiences in her lifetime, to give us some indication of the power and miracle that is our womanhood:

Puberty

DR MARY SHORT: "Two major hormonal stages occur during puberty. First the ovaries start to mature, body hair grows and breasts develop. Then you start to menstruate. For the first year-and-a-half most cycles are non-ovulating, so your periods will be irregular. There is nothing wrong with you when this occurs, it just

takes time for the system to adjust. It can be a difficult time for girls to see their bodies changing, often they get an excess distribution of female fat, in other words they might get a little pudgy, but that goes when they begin to ovulate. Dieting is not needed when girls are at this stage — it's part of development.

"I sometimes compare this stage to the menopause — young adolescents blush like crazy where menopausal women flush.

"Around the ages of 14/15/16 a women's hormones really take over. They get curious about sex, the physicality, the act. They can be easily aroused. They feel particularly charged-up around ovulation — that is nature's way of helping women to get pregnant. Obviously it is not advisable for them to get pregnant at this age so it is essential they understand and can manage their emotions.

"There is too much emphasis on contraception and not enough on sexuality in adolescent sex education. It is normal to be attracted to boys too, to be curious about sex, it's not something to feel embarrassed about. This is nature at work. It's so important to guide teenagers through this and help them not to confuse their raging hormones with deep emotional desire, lust with love. Seventeen and eighteen is when they are ready, hormonally and emotionally, to start to appreciate what a partner/boyfriend is about. You're really nurtured if you're made aware of what's happening hormonally at each of these physical stages.

"When girls start to establish regular cycles then other hormonal factors come into play."

Periods

It might help us to know, when we feel like tearing our hair out with premenstrual tension, that ovulation is more or less a monthly miracle.

DR MARY SHORT: "A message called FSH flies down from the brain to the ovary, ripens a follicle, which forms something like a shell on the egg. As soon as the FSH levels reach a certain height, the brain says 'Release the egg!' The egg reaches the tube ready to be fertilised.

"At the same time you produce lots of oestrogen which softens the neck of the womb so you get an increased discharge, which sperm love and which makes for an easy passage as it goes flying up to meet the egg.

"If you do not get pregnant your womb lining starts to come away — that's menstruation."

It might be a finely tuned hormonal process, but many women experience problems around their periods. Dr Mary Short looks at some of those problems and how to relieve them. She advises you to consult your doctor for advice about painful periods and PMS. Keep a diary of symptoms, but don't throw them all at once at your doctor. Prepare a list, discuss each topic on the list with your doctor. A list helps you to remember and to focus your thoughts.

Pre menstrual syndrome

MARY, 30s: *"I get premenstrual tension. My family have learned to ignore me when I fly off the handle, leave me alone when I burst into tears and not come near me when I have anything sharp in my hand! My husband actually dragged me to the doctor to get it sorted. Now I am on medication and I am a human being again for those red-letter days."*

AMANDA, 21: "I think the advertising executives who dream up tampon and sanitary towel adverts should be sacked. They're obviously all male. The truth is when I am due my period I suffer from depression, low self-esteem, back pain and I generally look like I've gone 10 rounds with Mike Tyson. I certainly don't feel like being pulled along on roller blades by a team of Dalmations. I went on the pill about a year ago which has really helped. I have taken oil of evening primrose too."

DR MARY SHORT: "Premenstrual syndrome is a group of symptoms which occur around the time of ovulation and are gone by the day of heaviest menstrual bleeding. The majority of women who experience PMS do so for five to seven days.

"Symptoms vary from breast tenderness and irritability, occasional bloating, to violent mood swings, irrational behaviour and an increase in domestic accidents. Milder symptoms may respond to Vitamin B6 or Evening Primrose Oil."

Dysmennorhoea

SIOBHAIN, 24: *"For two days a month I eat painkillers, feel ropey and go to sleep with hot water bottle against my stomach. Then the pain stops and I forget about it until the next time."*

DR MARY SHORT: "There two types of painful period — one is crampy and spasmodic in nature and the other is continuous pain — called congestive dysmennorhoea. The congestive type can happen as women get older and it may be due to having fibroids i.e. a thickening of the muscle in the womb.

"The most common cause of dysmennorhoea is hormonal and the periods tend to be crampy in nature. This is common in adolescent's periods and often resolves as we get older. Years ago it was treated by painkillers and, if they did not work, then a D & C, a scraping of the lining of the womb. Nowadays it is generally treated with medication specifically for period pain, or by preventing ovulation with the oral contraceptive pill."

Amennorhea

MARINA, 25: *"I only get a period once a year. I've had examinations by a gynaecologist but I have been told there is nothing they can do. I don't know if I can have children or not. I have been asked to come back when I want to try for a baby. I hear other women complaining about their periods and I wish I could have the same complaint. It's very upsetting."*

DR MARY SHORT: "Amennorhea literally means no periods. There are two types, one where you never get a period — that's primary — and the other where periods stop for no apparent reason. This is called secondary amennorhea.

"Primary amennorhea suggests either a physical or hormonal cause . The commonest cause of secondary amennorhea is pregnancy. But it can also occur with rapid weight loss, as in anorexia or in stressful circumstances."

Endometriosis

NOELLE, 34: *"I had painful periods and the pain was all day everyday during menstruation. The doctors told me it was endometriosis. Since I've had my baby it hasn't been half as bad."*

DR MARY SHORT: "The lining of the womb is called the endometrium — it grows and regresses each month. It can actually seed outside the womb and these areas are also under hormonal influence. They act as mini-wombs at the time of menstruation and bleed too. This eventually causes problems such as adhesion, or sticking to, the bowel, womb, ovaries and bladder. If you experience pain with this it generally lasts for the entire period of menstruation. Very severe cases may be a cause of infertility.

"Endometriosis can be managed by controlling the ovulation, or giving anovulatory cycles."

Menopause — the second adolescence

The menopause marks far more than a change in hormone levels — it is a passage to a new phase of your life, a phase in which childbearing and rearing is over and there are new challenges to face. Many women find themselves reflecting on the first half of their lives at the time of the menopause, and deciding what to do with the rest.

ALANNAH, 50s: "My periods changed, I started hot flushes. I didn't feel great, I found my mood changed and I was more vulnerable to life. Then I started to do things for myself, exercising regularly, reading. Another thing I do now is meditation.

"I took HRT for a time, but it didn't suit me. So now I use a cream instead. The night sweats and flushes are a thing of the past. Maybe it is just me, but I feel much more energetic since I came off HRT.

"When you have six children you don't feel sad at the loss of your fertility. I suppose sometimes you wish that you had those times again, to maybe not have them one after the other and with more time to enjoy them. I would hate to go back to all that mucking and messing again. I would certainly recommend exercise, it is terribly important, it is fabulous for your mind as well as your body. Keep interested in yourself."

ANN, 40s, had her womb and ovaries removed at 34.

"I was post menopausal overnight, that was hard. It's a major operation, having a hysterectomy, even though they are so common. It took me a while to recover. I'm on HRT and I'm as healthy as the day is long. If I had no money I would borrow it for HRT.

"It took me five years to realise that the days I'm down are the days I would have been getting my period. You need a lot of family support, to help you along. After hysterectomy you can look forward to a better life. You are not going to suffer with bad period pain and it doesn't affect your sex life, in my experience. If the ovaries aren't taken away, you still have a chance of going through your normal menopause.

"It is worthwhile being informed about hysterectomy, some of the women I know got together and wrote a booklet with the Health Promotion Unit. That's available for any woman, free of charge."

Hormone replacement therapy

DR MARY SHORT: "HRT is not an elixir of youth, but I do feel it alleviates a lot of the physical symptoms of menopause, notably flushes, vaginal dryness, i.e. dryness during intercourse, which is seldom talked about, but can be quite painful because there is no oestrogen to lubricate and the tissues get thin and papery."

MAGDALEN BRISTOW, a nurse, runs menopause workshops in the greater Dublin area, she has a lot to offer the women of Ireland going through this time — the second adolescence:

"When I am doing a course with women on the menopause I say: 'There is no point in us getting into this area until we see how you feel about yourself first. Because it is a time of change — a time of re-assessing your whole life.' Then we start to have a lot of fun and do a lot of serious work on self-image.

"The key to negotiating the menopause is to see it as something positive. It is the diving board into the deep end — the next part of your life. A freer part, a part where you have the experience to cope with the changes and the wisdom to wait until the right moment comes along to do things. Value your years. See the pitfalls you have come through and you might just see this hormonal change as something you're very capable of managing, if not enjoying.

"We start with the very basics: 'Can you change a light bulb?' They look at me in amazement. I send them away that week to change a light bulb or a plug or some task like that they have never considered doing before. Next week I ask them if they can change the wheel of a car. Each week they have to do something to become more independent. And the more independent you are the greater your self esteem.

"I come from a generation of women who were taught, more or less, as soon as you reach the menopause you should sit in the corner with a bag over your head. But that is changing by the week. I sometimes have to give talks to men who are finding it hard to cope with their menopausal wives — not because they are so hard to handle but because they have become different. They have become themselves.

"That is not because they are on Hormone Replacement Therapy, it is because they are beginning to realise just because they have been through the change does not mean they have to stop being female.

"My main point in running these menopause workshops is not just 'What are my oestrogen and progestogen levels?' It's 'What's going on in one's mind and body?' Each week one of the participants has an aromatherapy massage. Immediately you get a hesitancy — 'Am I going to have to take my clothes off in front of these other women?' I assure them it's only neck and shoulders. By week five they are clamouring to be next.

"We start to explore feelings. How does your partner feel about you doing this course? How do you feel about your partner? When you look at him what do you see? I give them one quote, among many: 'I'm important because God don't make no rubbish'.

"Because I am of a similar age group I can really relate to them and what they're feeling. In a lot of instances I have felt it myself."

Coping with the change

Emotionally, how do you cope with the vast hormonal changes going on during menopause?

MAGDALEN: "For every woman who is having difficulty going through the menopause, she will have two friends who are going through it quite easily and perhaps another friend who is sailing through it. She will feel guilty because she is feeling so bad: 'Why am I like this?' Her partner will be losing the rag occasionally: 'You're not the woman I married!'

"So, what we need to look at is what can be done on a positive basis. First they need a medical check up — for that I have the full backing of the Well Woman and the Woman's Medical Centre — to get their hormone levels balanced if necessary. Quite often their hormone levels are OK, it is a learned behaviour they are experiencing, or there are other events going on in their lives. They've heard the menopause is a nightmare so they expect to have one.

"Once they have been reassured that this is a natural process and they are more informed of the changes taking place in their body — their symptoms tend to diminish.

"A lot of problems experienced during the menopause might not necessarily have anything to do with it. We talk about that. I always encourage the other women to tell the others about themselves. Because they have so much to give. Just because I'm running the class does not mean I know it all. Nothing is more enlightening than personal experience and personal experience can be shared for the benefit of others.

"Also they are likely to be dealing with a man who is menopausal too! There isn't a medical male menopause but there's certainly a mid-life crisis."

Panic attacks

As MAGDALEN has mentioned, there are three ways of going through the menopause — some sail through it, most get by OK with a variety of symptoms, but a small percentage go through hell and find it hard to get sympathy because their friends aren't having the same symptoms.

MAGDALEN: "Hot flushes in public places, memories by association, these can lead to a build-up of anxiety. You are afraid it will happen again and the fear breeds a vicious circle.

"If you think you are having a panic attack, pop a sweet in your mouth if you feel faint to bring the blood sugar levels back up again. Try to slow down your breathing, concentrate on that. I would recommend anyone suffering with panic attacks get in touch with their doctor, read about the menopause, there are books available in every library and shop.

"Panic attacks undermine your confidence. If there are any courses or workshops on women's health and menopause in your area it would be worthwhile doing one."

Hot flushes

MAGDALEN: "I've sat in front of women with the sweat running off them insisting they're not menopausal because they're too young. And why shouldn't they feel afraid? They are at the end of the reproductive cycle of their life. It's all change again.

"On a practical level I advise them to carry moist tissues when they go out, they can keep them in the fridge or freezer and when they feel a flush they can put something ice cold on their skin.

"But, again we look at the emotional elements surrounding the hot flushes. If you think of the changes in terms of being positive rather than negative then you're laughing. You're actually going to have a lot more freedom than before. Once you're through it you won't suffer from premenstrual tension, period pains, pregnancy worries. You won't have to figure out times of the month.

"Post-menopausal women — what they have to give is incredible. Of course they may not be as pretty as they were at 20. But they're probably far more attractive — look at what they have to offer: a lifetime of experience! Life is great after The Change. I can tell you that from experience."

Make a wish...
Magdalen does this exercise with women in menopause workshops: Make a list of 10 things you've never done and wish to do and start working your way through them — starting with the easiest one first.

They don't have to be monumental — they can be a simple as going out for walks, buying yourself a CD, giving yourself a facial...

Further reading
What's Happening to My Body?
by Lynda Madaras
Penguin Books

Real Gorgeous
by Kaz Cooke
Bloomsbury

Menopause
by Dr Miriam Stoppard
Dorling Kindersley

Our Bodies Ourselves
by Jill Rakusen and Angela Phillips
Penguin

Woman's Experience of Sex
by Sheila Kitzinger
Penguin

Living with the Menopause
Medicine Education Group
62 Stert Street
Abingdon, Oxfordshire, UK

Chapter Thirteen

~~~~

SOMEWHERE OVER THE RAINBOW

"The more I learn about sexuality the less I know. It's such a deep, spiritual part of us and it is a lifelong, constantly evolving experience."
— **TRISH CAMERON**, Sexuality tutor and trainer.

WHAT DOES SEXUALITY MEAN TO US? How do we get in touch with it? How do we express it in a way that feels safe and right to us? All we really know about our sexuality is how we feel about it and ourselves, here and now. Sexuality is not the perfect orgasm or sexual technique, to be strived for and reached somewhere over the rainbow. Sex is one, important, way we express our sexuality. It is felt in so many other ways. It is who we are and what we are on this side of the rainbow — how we think and how we feel, laugh, cry, touch, bond, speak, make love, reflect and interact with all the things and people around us.

Sex and sexuality is not dirty. It is not something secretive or shameful. The aim of this chapter is to give you some indication of how women can express themselves, in many different ways, sexually. Their sexuality is not something divorced from the rest of them. Here some of the answers given to the question:

How do you view sex?

MARIE, 35: "It can be the closest you will ever get to another person and a very moving experience, depending on how you feel about your partner and yourself. On the other hand it can be just pleasurable fun."

RUTH, 18: "I think it is a very important part of a relationship. But it is often seen as purely physical with no emotional aspect."

DEBBIE, 37: "I was raped so it changed me. I am glad to have known beforehand how to pleasure myself — it helped! If sex is not an emotional experience or an intense fantasy experience it means very little."

SINEAD, 25: "I really believe it can very destructive. My generation seems to thrive on it. But they seem to have lost the real concept of love being a major part of it. However it is very pleasurable and I can see why people slip into sleeping around. But sleeping with someone you have got to know is a lot more of a sensual experience than shagging some stranger."

GWENDOLINE, 24: "It is an important part of a loving relationship, helping to create intimacy and besides it's fun."

ORLA, 32: "It's something mysterious and sensual — like eating delicious food."

JULIE, 37: "I like it but it's not the top of my list of priorities. We tend to have a lot of sex when on holiday but at home we sometimes forget to do it!"

DEBORAH, 29: "WOW!"

SINEAD, 21: "From as many different angles as I can think of."

FIONA, 45: "Something I am afraid of."

PAT, 31: "Over-rated."

ELAINE, 30: "An important part of my relationship with my husband."

MARGARET, 50: "I think it is a shame if people don't meet imaginative and caring lovers as it is not just about penetration. I have been very lucky."

VIOLET, 29: "Sex, for me, gets better all the time."

The answers are all so incredibly diverse, which makes sense since sexually we are all as unique, as we are in every other way.

This chapter looks at sexuality in the deepest sense of the word. Those reading it might feel there is a heterosexual bias. Most women are in heterosexual relationships. Therefore most of the women interviewed are heterosexual. But the insight and advice given is true for straight, gay, and bisexual women — however we choose to express our sexuality. **TRISH CAMERON**, whose quote opens this chapter with the most honest and telling truth about sexuality, has given workshops and counselled in the area for many years. She feels the more she learns the less she knows.

Yet she has a tremendous amount to teach those of us only beginning the journey — thanks to her years of insight and experience. She starts off from this premise:

"Everything you feel is OK. You have to allow yourself to feel it in order to find out who you really are...

"When we think of sexuality we usually think of sexual intercourse, but it so much more than that. If we take it right back to when we were born, the first thing people looked for was our sex. It starts right from there. Studies have shown that people talk and relate to baby girls differently than to baby boys. Conditioning sets in from the very start.

"Sexuality is your expression of who you are as a woman, maybe the way you walk, the way that you speak, the way you wash the dishes..."

How we relate to other people sexually

"Most of the time we go around with all our barriers up. But we are born out of sex and every interaction we have with people and with nature is in a way sexual. I don't mean sexual in terms of intercourse. I mean sexual in terms of being a human being, a female human being, a life force.

"Women have told me about sitting on the top of a mountain and walking by the sea, how the beauty of their surroundings inspires orgasmic feelings. They absorb the scenery as they would absorb a lover. The world is full of sexual energy.

"But because we are afraid, and have all our conditioning around sex, we generally don't feel what's around us. We are scared of opening up to other people. This repression is not good for us physically, mentally, or spiritually.

"Repression of sexuality is trying to suppress who you really are."

Trish advises women who want to explore their sexuality further to think about doing a course. But she would recommend you do personal development and assertiveness work first.

"The fact is it can cause tremendous upheaval in your life when you begin to explore your sexuality.

"Sexuality is not actually divorced from the rest of our lives. It is mirrored in our economic, social, political and spiritual upbringing. Society is made up of people and their sexuality. So getting in touch with it is bound to have repercussions in other aspects of your life."

ELLEN, 40s, ended up exploring her sexuality as part of her personal development and assertiveness training:

"I was 41 when I did that course, and up until then sex was something I didn't talk about. Sex for me was for reproduction, yet I am a very outgoing woman. I love life, so there was a total conflict between what I would like to have done with it and what was morally wrong.

"The word sexuality took on a whole new meaning for me. What it meant before was sex mainly and all things to do with sex. Then it transformed. My sexuality became the way that I dress, walk, move, what I like to eat, the wines I like to drink, all these things and more.

"We did a lot of work around the woman getting back into her body. We had to sit down and get different parts of our body to talk to us and listen to what they had to say. I never knew that my body knew what was good for itself. I now honestly believe my job is to listen to it.

"I am a married woman and our sex life was average. I had to find out what turned me on. So I took time out to find out. My husband and I didn't have much of a sex life at that time and I wound it down even further, because I just didn't know where I was. I was having sex to please him and I wasn't really happy with that.

"So I just explained to him that I needed time to myself for a while, on a sexual level, to sort things out. Then I found out about myself, my body, what I liked what I didn't like. I like being flattered, I like to be among people. I feel turned on when I get a compliment...I felt all those things.

"It worked for me.."

ALEX, 37, did a sexuality course a few years ago and found it opened doors to her that had been shut since childhood:

"I didn't know there was such a thing as a sexuality course until I decided to do a personal development/assertiveness course.

"What did I get out of it? The word for me would be liberation. I could only ever express my sexuality through another person. Having done the course, it made me realise sexuality is part of me and who I am. I can express it in any way that I choose.

"I had to realise that it is OK to massage your body, to do those things for yourself that I never felt comfortable about doing. I opened up to it immediately, it was just what I needed. I am a sexual person.

"I enjoy my body now. When I masturbate, I go upstairs, light the candles, give myself a nice bath, rub oils in afterwards. I would have masturbated before but it would have been very secretive and I would have felt guilty afterwards.

"Getting my first vibrator was a real landmark too. I would never have thought of a vibrator in any way other than 'that's what perverts use.' I use it to massage other parts of my body, not just for clitoral stimulation and penetration.

"Since the sexuality course I am a much stronger person. My sexuality is like a light inside of me. I feel alive again. Before, I feel, I was half-dead. The most sexual part of me is my mind."

Both Alex and Ellen have ended up teaching assertiveness, personal development and sexuality to other women. They are convinced the path they have taken will help other women unleash their sexuality and the power within themselves.

Affairs

Surveys show a greater number of married or committed women than ever will have an affair. Many would point to this as an indication that society is falling apart. But are all affairs necessarily bad for you? Here women talk about their experiences of either having affairs or living with an unfaithful partner.

JOJO, 32: "There was another man in my life that I liked, and who certainly turned me on. At first I was frightened of that but I made sense of it. My needs were not being met. So I pursued the relationship for a while, and it took great courage to do that. It was wonderful, we had a very good relationship.

"I did not tell my husband. My husband and I are now working on our relationship. I don't need sex as often as he would like me to, so we are working on that.

"I felt that this road was waiting for me to travel it. I have come into myself. I think that women get depressed because they don't feed their physical side, they are even ashamed to say they have a need."

JENNIFER, 35: "I have recently finished an affair which went on for about a year. I felt it was part of a process that I was going through at the time, and I enjoyed it. I learned a lot from it and I didn't feel guilty.

"I don't think it is natural to be faithful. I am 35 now and I would feel stifled if I felt that I couldn't go out and have more experiences. Having the affair has given me confidence and furthered my exploration into my sexuality."

LARA, 28: "I've had a number of affairs since I got married and started living with my partner. I feel that I am playing with fire and I cannot stop myself. It's important to me that the man makes the first move, then I can say 'I couldn't help myself, he wouldn't leave me alone.' My husband suspects and I feel he will find out. If he does he will be devastated. He really loves me and I love him. I just don't feel secure in myself — that's why I need this approval from other men.

"It's also the high. At the moment it's worth feeling like shit after. I am actively seeking a sex therapist. This can't go on."

MARGARET, 46: "I put up with my husband being unfaithful for years. There came a stage when I had to sit down with pen and paper and write out the benefits of staying in the marriage against the benefits of getting out. When I saw one was longer than the other I knew it was time for me to say 'enough'.

"So I asked him to leave.

"The benefits of my decision are still a longer list. Having a decent night's sleep — knowing you're not going to be woken at five in the morning by the door opening and him creeping in, pretending he was there all night, makes it worthwhile."

TRIONA, 38: "I found my partner had been unfaithful to me, which upset me as I am a very loyal person. I put fidelity first. The fact she had been dishonest with me, was harder to bear than the fact she had been with another woman. She made it very hard for me to trust anyone again. But then I realised — our love had died a long time ago and it was just her way of moving on.

"Because she had not the guts to make a clean break she used someone else. I imagine her new girlfriend will find it hard to trust her given the fact she knows she is capable of cheating. Whereas I know no matter how bad the relationship is going I wouldn't want it to end that way."

BETTY, 42: "I will love my husband always, but I couldn't take him having an affair when I was eight months pregnant. We had a good relationship up until that point, but he drank. We went for counselling but the drink stopped him from treating it seriously. He had to stay in denial about everything. I loved him but I let him go because I love myself more."

I want to break free

There are many other reasons why women decide they do not want to be with their long-term partners anymore. But many have their root in the need to explore themselves, and sexuality has a part to play in that.

NOELLE, 26, feels she has a lot to learn about herself emotionally and sexually before she makes a commitment again:

"I finished with someone recently. Even though we went out together for a few months we did not discuss the issue of his impotence or his lack of sexual experience.

"Sex was totally disappointing and anything other than me lying on the flat of my back was out of the question. Also everything always had to be on time, if we were going somewhere he was always clock-watching and I was always anxious.

"But then it occurred to me that, having been involved with another difficult man for a long time, I just wanted to have sex with none of the complications. I wanted to concentrate on my sexuality for a while without having the worry of coping with someone else's. I have to say it was very liberating to be that nice and thoughtful to myself."

Do I really want sex?

"Anything goes it seems, except celibacy." — Sheila Kitzinger 'Woman's Experience of Sex.'

Many women find periods of celibacy are important to reflect and tune into your sexuality, without the confusion of involvement.

CATHERINE, 35, was celibate after ending a four-year relationship:

"I took a conscious decision to stay celibate for at least six months. I learned more about my sexuality in that period than any other time of my life, particularly about what I wanted from life and a partner. When, nine months later, I found someone I wanted to make love with again I was not carrying ghosts. I was me."

TRISH CAMERON: "I think choosing celibacy for a period of time can be very beneficial in exploring your own sexuality. If it's a positive choice it's great. Our conditioning often tells us if you do not have someone you will fall apart. In fact it can be very empowering to know you can feel whole alone, that is once you are not withdrawing out of fear of being involved and getting hurt. Avoiding sex because you're frightened is something you need to work through and understand."

Touch

Touch is important in learning how to communicate with people. But for some women there is a very definite problem in distinguishing physical contact from sex:

SIOBHAIN, 29: "I grew up in a house in which hugging and physical contact had no part. It left me feeling very starved of affection. Sex was a huge discovery for me, but I had sex for affection a lot of the time. I gave out signals to men and was not in control of myself. I ended up being very hurt and I also ended up getting involved with men who I was not attracted to, because they offered me attention and affection. It took a lot of work and psychotherapy to make me realise I don't have to have sex with every man. I have sex when I want it and with the people I want to have it with. That's a gift."

JUDITH ASTON is a massage therapist and psychotherapist, she helps many women to realise not all touch has to be sexual:

"The body has been so marginalised, the body is seen as dirty and should be hidden and not touched and not celebrated or enjoyed. We need support, satisfaction, appreciation, we need T.L.C., we need intimacy with other people. Touch is a key way to develop people's growth or expression.

"You may not know that you want non-physical sexual touch, so you settle for sexual touch, because you couldn't say to the person 'I just want you to hold me and hug me and love me.'"

Staying faithful

MARY-ANN, 70s: "I don't come from this generation, where you all talk about your private life. My private life with my husband, who died last year, will remain private. But

I will say this. We had a 51-year marriage in which we stayed faithful and loving to each other. That's an achievement. One of the biggest of my life. Now that didn't just happen. that took a lot of work. And that's what people need to put into their marriages today — work."

TRISH CAMERON: "People tend not to think about it seriously enough before they promise it. Society has changed an awful lot since the days when we had clearly defined roles to slot into and therefore it was easier to promise 'Till death us do part'. You have to view the commitment you're getting into and decide whether you're capable of it. It is a pledge and it might not suit your relationship needs at the moment.

"I believe I have the capacity to stay faithful but I don't actually know if I can be for the rest of my life. I can only say I will try. Again you have to decide what is important to you, and remember to accept yourself as you are in making that decision. Do you really know what 'for better or for worse' means? Are you prepared for what it entails?"

JODIE: "Catherine and I, we are not really into pieces of paper so it doesn't bother us that as lesbians we cannot have a state-recognised ceremony. It just makes us more aware of our commitment as a changing thing, evolving on a daily basis. All we know is we are in love now. And want to stay this way"

Guilt and judgement

JUDGEMENT

TRISH CAMERON: "Judging people by your own sexual standards is perhaps one of the the biggest wrongs in our society. If you judge others you are not being fair."

GUILT

We live in a world of whisper and innuendo where sex is concerned. Huge myths grow up around it. We are made to feel guilty when we're having sex and, amazingly, we're made to feel guilty when we're not having it! We live in a society which sells everything from washing machines to cars to bottles of trendy lager using sex. They feed on our own dissatisfaction and promote sex as the cure all — buy this dress or this make up or this new motor and you'll attract hoards of admirers... We all end up being obsessed over sex.

TRISH CAMERON: "You have to break down the obsessions, see it as something normal, usual, a part of life. How can we be in real control of something we're either guilty or obsessed about?

"When I teach sex education as part of a life-skills programme in schools and other institutions, I tell people what we are talking about is as normal as peeling spuds for the dinner, doing your maths homework, going shopping.

"We don't suddenly become sexual beings when we are legally allowed to do it at 16. We are evolving sexually from the time we are born. But by not telling young people about it, in detail, we are making them curious about something they know nothing about and therefore cannot make informed decisions upon."

A good way of regaining control over your sexuality is to begin to acknowledge the guilt and obsessions and judgements within yourself. Write them out if you can and then look out for ways of letting it go — by doing courses or counselling or even something as simple as sharing your thoughts with a friend. You might find this difficult, even frightening.

We have every reason of being afraid to do this because:

TRISH CAMERON: "Guilt and obsession are about protection because as long as we feel them we don't have to face up to who we really are. Nelson Mandela said something very profound which can be applied to our sexuality: 'It is not our darkness we are afraid of it is our light.'

"Guilt, fear and obsession are excuses not to show the beauty and goddess within because we can't believe we can really be so loveable and powerful."

LONG-TERM LOVER and PASSING FANCY

In an ideal world we would all love to adore our partners passionately until the day we die.

In a long-term relationship sex can really become staid and dull if it is not worked on. But you can regenerate sexual interest:

TRISH CAMERON: "The charge between you can neutralise, of course. You don't necessarily have to go off and have intercourse with someone else who you find attractive to get it back. You are in charge of your sexuality, you don't have to give it away to every man or woman who finds you attractive. At the same time don't deny you feel attracted to people just because you're married. If you do, the combination of a few drinks and that feeling may overwhelm you and you might act in a way you will regret the next day.

"Again it is conditioning which says 'If I fancy someone I have to sleep with.' You can feel all the feelings, let them enrich you. You are a sexual being and entitled to feel the fire inside. That is who you are and you don't stop feeling attraction for other people as soon as you have a sparkler or gold band on your finger. You are still gorgeous and as desirable as ever."

BLUSHING

SUZANNE, 28: *"I have a terrible problem in that I blush every time I talk to an attractive man. It's so obvious I fancy him."*

TRISH CAMERON: "Allow yourself to blush. He'll be flattered by it. Sexuality is supposed to be fun. In Ireland we take it so seriously. It's all so heavy. Blushing is a very beautiful reaction. If it's not possible to follow the attraction through physically you might even want to follow it through mentally the next time you masturbate. You're not hurting anyone by doing that. You're not causing anyone pain and you're giving yourself pleasure. If you allow yourself to have the feelings they usually pass. If not they become distorted."

I AM MY MOTHER'S DAUGHTER

We may regard ourselves as more sexually liberated than our mothers and, in terms of society's changing and moving on, we probably are. However if you are any way honest you will begin to realise there is a lot more influence on you than you are conscious of and that is what is known as conditioning. No member of society grows up without it. You have to be aware of this in order to start reclaiming who you are:

NORA, 29: "I was 10. I was playing on the beach, with my cousins who were younger than me, when they all took off their wet togs and were running naked through the sand dunes to get warm. I stripped off to join them, I was after all one of the children. When my father caught sight of me he said 'Nancie,' my mother 'tell Nora to but her clothes back on.'

"I felt instantly ashamed of myself. The cold damp of the costume was like a reminder I had done something wrong in showing my body. I sat there shivering and feeling guilty, neither a child or an adult. There was no-one else like me. I was completely alone. I think I've felt that way for a lot of my life."

JOSEPHINE, 66: "I have a very loving relationship with my husband and I enjoy sex. I really like it. But I grew up in an era where it was immodest to show any part of your body. I go to an aerobics for over 60s class and when we are in the changing room I still undress under a towel. I would love to feel able to walk naked into the showers. A lot of women do but some of them wear swimsuits."

Have you got the time?

For most of us sex is a night-time occupation just before lights out, except on the weekends and even then if you have children it's done with the chair against the door, or an eye on the clock in case they wake up.

BARBARA, 46: "My fella makes love like he's learning how to waltz — he's concentrating heavily and going '1-2-3, 1-2-3'. I wish to God sometimes he could let go!"

MAGGIE, 39: "We never make love outside the bedroom. I think I'd like to try someplace else."

TRISH CAMERON: "Why on earth do we leave sex until the end of the day! Many women are literally too tired. They've been running around all day minding kids, are out at work or both.

"How on earth are you supposed to generate enough energy for a sexual experience?

"Sex is an important act. For me if I am going to come to it I am going to come to it with all my senses intact. I want to fully participate in it and be alert.

"I know there are logistical difficulties but it should not be some ould thing we do at the end of the day just before we snuff out the candle.

"It should be given the respect and enthusiasm deserves. And the time.

"Be honest, be intimate, with the person you are with."

FANTASIES

TRISH CAMERON: "Fantasy is great, it can be a very good kick-start and add excitement to your sex life.

"The only danger is when you fantasise all the time to the extent that your lover is not part of it. If you're constantly thinking about someone else and being somewhere else you are not present in the moment and with your lover.

"But occasionally we do need it. Maybe the sheets need changing or your partner has just eaten garlic!

"Sex is real. We don't have perfect bodies or move as smoothly and passionately through the act as they make out on the big and little screen. We don't all have partners who look like the handsome hero on television. We only have ourselves and each other.

"You can share fantasy in order to include your lover: 'Imagine we're on a deserted island with nothing but palm trees for shelter... There's nothing wrong in that, once you both enjoy it."

Masturbation

SHEILA, 26: "It does zilch for me. I can't get aroused without another person's involvement.'

JANET, 32: "I can't do it. I feel like my dead granny is watching from above!"

MIRIAM, 49: "I learned how to masturbate late in life and now it seems I can't do without it. I use it to relax, to arouse. The only real difficulty is I don't find sex with my partner as enjoyable. I need to be able to arouse myself."

A lot of the comments on masturbation from women seemed to centre around their inability to be turned on by it. Why?

TRISH CAMERON: "Women have been told it is wrong, a mortal sin, not right. It's an important part of self-expression. Again if you're doing it constantly you have to watch out — you are escaping in some way. You can get locked into it, like anything, to avoid something else. Maybe there are feelings coming up you don't want to deal with.

"Sometimes women are very afraid of the images that come into their heads when they masturbate. We are a mish-mash of different character types so it's OK to fantasise about different things. You have to gain the ability to say 'This is what I am experiencing, I'll not judge it, I'll let it be OK.' Fantasies come and go, when you're conscious of them and in charge. If you repress them they come back and may have greater control over you.

"Masturbation is time to be with yourself, to luxuriate in your sense of you and your imagination and ability to pleasure and arouse yourself.

"It's a very important part of a sexuality course. We talk about it very honestly and openly."

Experimentation

Am I straight? Am I gay? Am I both? Some women decide to try sex with both sexes to find out more about their sexuality:.

KATHERINE, 25: "For me sexuality is your propensity to have sex and the openness and willingness around it.

"I'm not promiscuous, but I have done things to find out what they are like rather than relying on hearsay and innuendo. I had a sexual experience with another woman, a friend. She is a really sensual person, we had been dropping hints about it before and then it just happened one night. The sex was not great at all. But it was exciting to think about it afterwards and I would like to try it again. I'm not gay — I'm just curious."

Loving women

EMMA, 27, is gay: "A few of my straight friends tell me they have had one-off experiences with the same sex. They have discreet liaisons which they don't label sexually as anything but experiment. However there is a distinct difference when you realise it is for you. It's just the most natural, electric experience in the world.

"Ireland has changed massively in terms of lesbian awareness — still not as much as it could but it's very encouraging for me.

"I knew I was lesbian at 14 and eventually came out at college in 1989. The atmosphere then was much more scary and guarded than it is now. Coming out to the public is not as bad as coming out to your mother — what do I care what the public think? My mother's reaction was wonderful: understanding, open.

"I'm lucky in that I came from a very supportive background. I had everything going for me except for this one huge difference, which I had to keep closeted until such time as they wouldn't send me off to a psychiatrist for evaluation.

"I was in a relationship in school. It was very covert and quite terrifying in case we were caught. I just remember the fear and isolation — mainly because of social pressure. I was very much afraid my friends would despise me. The thing about being lesbian is you are never suspected, you won't be outed which makes it very tempting to stay in the closet.

"For the benefit of others still in the closet I will say I got a huge burst of energy and sense of relief from coming out. My family were supportive. I know now I was brought up in the ideal family and situation for it. If you live in a small rural area it is not so easy. Call one of the helplines and let them help you. [see directory]

"There is support there. There are local groups all over the place and no matter how fearful you are there is no place worse than the closet. We all carry the scars. It's a dark, claustrophobic, horrific place. It has left me with a horror of secrets

"I express my love for my girlfriend publicly. I always have. But it's as if a red siren starts flashing on top of your head. Here I am, stretching out my arm and kissing my girl-friend in a spontaneous display of affection, which of course can take the spontaneity away. But it is one light that I cling to. I have been heckled because of it.

"It's OK to grieve for the traditional upbringing you had. Society gives us so many pats on the back for being conventional — if you do stray from the path it takes those pats back. That can be lonely.

"You don't have to declare and define your sexuality at any given age. For a lot of people it changes. I don't think I am bisexual but I try to keep an open mind on it. I think people should do that — it saves them defining their sexuality so completely, and then finding a bit that doesn't fit.

"And the sex? It's out of this world — and I really mean it can take you out of this world and into another. I don't drink or smoke. I find sex gives me all the stimulus I need."

The good lover

How does finding ourselves help us to become good lovers, and to find good lovers?

TRISH CAMERON: "A key to dismantling sexual barriers is finding a partner who we feel safe with and are attracted to.

"I think, fundamentally, the Irish are very gutsy, earthy, sexual people, we're also very spiritual.

"Sometimes it is too terrifying to expose yourself in that very intimate act of sex and loving. We erect barriers around ourselves without even being conscious of them. We think we are being open but to be open can get you hurt, so you close that part of yourself off, when you close yourself off you close sexuality.

"The challenge for us as women is to take the journey back to who you are, to *Being You*, to allow you to shine through again. This affects your sexuality because you are your sexuality.

"We have a big division in Ireland between the Mother and the Lover. Some women really want to hold onto the nurturing mother side of themselves. So they'll nurture their men, but they aren't the Lover, so the sexual part of that relationship can wither away.

"The Mother role has positive sides of course, she's the nurturer and life giver, the creator. But she is only part of the whole woman, the whole you. Giving the Mother total power in your psyche is to become compulsive and negative. You will try to control everything.

"This is what happens with certain Irish women, they lay down the law: 'I am in charge of the house. I am in charge of the children's upbringing.' You can end up holding onto your children too tightly. Even your husband becomes your son and you can't truly express your sexuality with him if he's in the son's role.

"The women who do this are not intentionally domineering, they are simply attaching too strongly to their families out of fear of being themselves. Passion is dampened.

"We need the lover, she is vital to our expression of who we are. But again, if you become too much the lover you are using sex to fill a black hole inside you. It cannot fill it completely. You feel good for five minutes or days and then you need to fill it again. That is hunger, addiction. No man or sexual partner can fill you up completely."

What we need is a good working relationship between the 'Mother' and the 'Lover'. The two being able to co-exist withinus so that we can draw on either at will.

Bartering

TRISH CAMERON: "Women throughout the ages have bartered sex for security and financial support. In one way it's an extreme length to go to to get your needs met. But, so long as you're aware of what you're doing that's OK, but if you're doing it to compensate for something else it is a very unhappy place to be."

Fairytale sexuality is played out in real life, with Hollywood lovers posing cosily for *Hello!* magazine, revealing to the world how they've found the fulfillment in each other that they never found in their previous three marriages. Sheila Kitzinger has written extensively on female sexuality. In her book *Woman's Experience of Sex* (Penguin, £9.99) she has this to say:

"Underlying the glossy photographs ......is the story of ... those apparently most fortunate of women held up as an example to the rest of us....like Princess Diana, film stars and the wives of millionaires. Men are perceived in terms of their work and achievements. Women have a social role and identity merely because of their relationships with men, and the sexual tie [of this] defines who a woman is...

"... In spite of the changes in sexual fashions, women are still expected to 'settle down' eventually, with a clearly defined sexual tie with one man. The Cosmo girl or 'liberated' woman can enjoy varied sexual relationships for a few years, but by the age of 30 or so, even she has to watch out if she is not to be seen to be on the road to becoming an 'embittered old maid'."

How does this translate to ordinary, everyday, female life?

TRISH CAMERON: "Some women have learned to allow or offer sex in return for something else — the living room painted etc. Not because they want it and enjoy it. The notions is: "I'm doing it because I'm putting up with it because I want something out of it. You're entitled to it twice a week."

Of course we don't do it consciously, but perhaps we need to look at why we think some women have it made because they 'land' a wealthy man.

And if we do find ourselves admitting to having thought that, there is no reason why we shouldn't we've been taught to think like that. Cinderella, Sleeping Beauty, Little Women... our storybooks are full of the notion we will be truly happy with a wealthy, handsome prince.

TRISH CAMERON: 'Thankfully this perception is changing. We see a lot of men helping women to achieve their inner hopes and dreams. We have to remember to acknowledge them for that. No matter whether the man or the woman is forging ahead successfully, the supportive, silent partner is as important as the successful one, whether it be a man or a woman."

Sex guides

They can be very valuable to couples or individuals learning about lovemaking but a great many of these 'How to' books concentrate on the technique and tend to ignore the emotions involved in lovemaking.

TRISH CAMERON: "In our society we tend to leave out the emotional component in most aspects of life. Everything is performance orientated. Why should sex be seen any differently? Sex manuals reflect this.

"Our education system doesn't really concentrate on emotional development. Although schools are now beginning to develop life-skills programmes they are still not emphasised enough. So when it comes to expressing our sexuality it can be seen as something we can achieve and pin down by reading a few books and articles. Hey presto!

"For me the joy of sexuality is knowing all those feelings I feel inside are actually mine. They are not because of anyone else. Once I let go of the guilt I can revel in my feelings. My body is re-sensitised and when that happens you can really come from the heart

"Whoever sat you down and said: 'Right, you are going to be a woman and you need to be taught about the art of making love?

"Nobody. That's because nobody ever talked about it until recently so nobody knew what anyone else was doing. We went into the most intimate expression of our beings blind, cold, without knowledge. We were supposed to be experts. It's not possible."

Sexuality and spirituality

"...God moves in passion. And since you are a breath in God's sphere, a leaf in God's forest, you too should rest in reason and move in passion." — **KAHLIL GIBRAN** 'The Prophet'

Most of us grew up in a religious tradition which had a lot to say about controlling sexual urges and very little about allowing your sexual expression to develop along with the rest of you. But as far as Trish Cameron is concerned, the two go hand in hand.

"In our tradition we are taught that God is in the sky. To be close to Him we have to disassociate with earthly things. Spirituality is not seen as part of the earth — it is a concept, despite the fact Christ was a very real man with a big heart.

"I believe there are seven main power points in the body, known as the the Chakras, which channel the life force through us. The first one is the sexual chakra at the base of your spine — it is the spark of creation. From that everything else is built upon so if you are closed off in your base chakra you can't act openly in all the others. If you're cut off sexually it is difficult to love, and we all want love in our lives.

"One of the greatest learning experiences for me was recognising and appreciating that sexuality and spirituality are part of each other. Once you start taking care of yourself and your body you are doing a very spiritual thing."

If you find this hard to believe you have only to look at the Bible to find some of the most beautiful tributes to sexuality ever written. This one, from the Song of Songs, is often chosen for a wedding reading:

SONG OF SONGS 4:1-4. 5:
How beautiful you are, my beloved, how beautiful you are!
Your eyes are doves, behind your veil;
Your hair is like a flock of goats surging down Mount Gilead.
Your teeth, a flock of sheep to be shorn, when they come up from the washing.
Each one has its twin, not one unpaired with another.
Your lips are a scarlet thread and your words enchanting.
Your cheeks, behind your veil, are halves of pomegranate......
.....Verses 10-16
My love is fresh and ruddy to be known among 10,000.
His head is golden, purest gold.
His eyes are like doves beside the water courses, bathing themselves in milk,
perching on a fountain-rim.
His cheeks are beds of spices, banks sweetly scented.
His lips are lillies, distilling pure myrrh.
His hands are golden, rounded, set with jewels of tarshish.
His belly a block of ivory covered with sapphires.
His legs are alabaster columns set in sockets of pure gold.
His appearance is that of Lebanon, unrivalled as the cedars.
His conversation is sweetness itself, he is altogether loveable.
Such is my love, such is my friend, oh daughters of Jerusalem.
If you find the biblical language hard going OK, but you can still how sexuality is seen as a cele-
bration of life and love and a part of our religious traditions -not something separate or
uninvolved."

Sex and disability

MARION: 'I have no feeling in the genital area but I have plenty of feeling everywhere else. Just watching someone make love to you in those areas where you are desensitised is stimulating, because it is so visual and sexually powerful."

Sex for those with disabilities can be hard to discover, mainly because the nature in which many of those who were now adults with disabilities grew up was one that did not lend itself to privacy.

AMY, 33: contracted polio at a young age and uses a wheelchair:

"Sexual development for a lot of people my age and older 'with disabilities' has been hampered by living in institutions. I lived in one myself at one time and it is dehumanising. There is no privacy. If you are lined up 'virtually naked' in line for communal showers it is hard to get a notion of your body being your own.

"Also a lot of people who worked in these institutions would have regarded us as sexless. I was caught reading *Dear Daughter* by a teacher who basically demanded to know what someone the likes of me was doing reading such a thing. It wasn't for the likes of me.

"I never believed I was any different to able-bodied people and I enjoy a loving, active sex life. But I can see why those with disabilities, who spent a long time in institutions, would."

Physical problems

CATRIONA, 45: "For the first three years of my marriage I couldn't physically make love. If I had not had an understanding husband I doubt that I would be married today. There was no one to help at that time, to give advice. It was the most lonely, awful feeling."

Vaginismus, involuntary clenching of the vaginal muscle, is much more common than women think. Many sufferers think they are the only women in the world to go through it. **BONNIE MAHER**, a sex therapist, works alongside Dr Eimer Phibin Bowman, running a clinic for sexual difficulties at the Well Woman Centre in Dublin:

"There are women who have a psychosomatic problem with clenching of the vaginal muscle. Actually some of them have very rich sex lives, orgasmic sex, oral sex, masturbation, great intimacy, no problems around nudity. But they are just terrified of the pain of penetration.

"The fear of pregnancy and childbirth is huge among patients too. Sometimes these women have had some sort of trauma, perhaps a doctor with the rubber gloves investigating when they were too young to understand and were frightened of it. Very often the behavioural approach works very well with these women.

"I'm referring to the woman who does have sexual feelings and longs for full, penetrative sex. Whereas the woman who comes in and says she has no sexual drive, has never fancied anybody, has no libido, has never tried to masturbate — it is much harder to help. But these women are not alone either.

"I find Irish women in general are very good at talking about sex. The real display of courage is actually making the appointment. Then the only way to deal with it is to be very direct and use the proper language.

"I work with women who are not in a relationship too. Although I do think it is not just a woman's problem, they can do a lot of work on their own. When I hear the woman saying that it is her problem and not her partner's, then I insist on seeing both of them. The age range of clients is as wide as the sexually active years. I have had one very recently, who was only 17.

"There are some sad cases. I had one woman who had been married 19 years and she had never had penetrative sex. That was a very sad story, she had been through an awful lot over the years. She had been through shock therapy as a result of vaginismus. I think her self-esteem really suffered.

"Her husband was a wonderful man, together they had worked out their own acceptance of it. It was too late for her to have children. For a lot of people wanting a baby is the big motivator.

"My advice to any woman suffering with vaginismus, or any other sexual problem, is to contact the Well Woman. You don't have to suffer alone and you are not the only one.

1. Staying sexually centred

In this exercise you will call on some of the images our pre-Celtic ancestors used to express different emotions and aspects of their personality. Although it has been adapted it still bears a resemblance to the ritual our foremothers probably carried out thousands of years ago.

Close your eyes. Draw a circle around yourself and stand in the centre. Now place four imaginary women at the edge of the circle. Each is an equal distance away from you. In the middle is you — the woman you are. If you feel pulled to one particular image concentrate on placing yourself in the centre once more.

Don't be alarmed by the fact that two of the images are negative. We all have shadows or dark sides, which must be acknowledged.

NURTURING WOMAN
Cares, creates, nurtures. Gives life. She feeds and gives birth to the next generation. She is the mother and carer in us.

RIGID WOMAN
Has given too much of herself, without being replenished. Care has turned to needing and starts to drain energy, She feels bitter . She is no longer soft and nurturing, she is rigid.

RAINBOW WOMAN
Creative, she is very into expression of who she is. Has tremendous passion and love. Creative energy is sexual energy, we are made out of creation.

LOST WOMAN

Creativity and passion are blocked. She is depressed through lack of expression.

She has been hurt and therefore her expression of her sexuality is hampered or withdrawn altogether.

Face and feel all these women in turn, allowing them to be a part of you.

Remember you are not one or all of these images, they are stereotypical. If you are more one of these women than the other, set aside a few minutes each day to pull yourself mentally back into the centre of the circle. Remember — none of these women have an exclusive right to you.

2. Daydream believer

Some of us might have a problem with sexual fantasising or erotic literature. So let's create our own fantasies which can go as far as we want or stop as soon as we feel comfortable. You might only want to go as far as dreaming up a scenario which culminates in you being kissed passionately, or exchanging a loaded look across a crowded room. That's still a powerful expression of sexuality.

You might want to be the mistress of Fionn MacCumhail or a space-age woman making love en route to Mars, or Cleopatra luxuriating in ass's milk and adorning herself for a night of passion with handsome Anthony. You might be on a beach in the Bahamas or on top of a Kerry mountain or in a huge four-poster bed...

The possibilities are endless. Take pen and paper and write it down if you really want to keep the image.

Everyone has a right to daydream or night-dream. Why not you?

Further reading
The Mirror Within
by Anne Dickson
Quartet Books

A Woman's Experience of Sex
by Sheila Kitzinger
Penguin

My Secret Garden
by Nancy Friday
Hutchinson

Coming Out in Ireland
by Suzy Byrne and Junior Larki
Marina Books

The Directory

A

A.I.M.S.
(Association for Improvements in the Maternity Services)
Berna Hanrahan
Raheen House
Meath Road
Bray
Co Wicklow
Ph: 01-2829447

Addiction Treatment
Rutland Centre Ltd
Knocklyon House
Knocklyon Rd
Dublin 16
Ph: 01-4946358/4946972

Aids for Parents under Stress
Cathedral St
Dublin 1
Ph: 01-8742066

Aids Helpline
Dublin 1
Ph: 01-8724277

Alexandra College Guild
Alexandra College
Milltown
Dublin 6
Ph: 01-4977571

ALONE
Willie Bermingham Place
Dublin 8
Ph: 01-6791032

Alternative Medicine
42 Crumlin Road
Dublin 12
Ph: 01-4730394

Altrusa
265 Collins Avenue
Whitehall
Dublin 9

An Post Womens Network
GPO, O'Connell St
Dublin 1
Ph: 01-7057275

Aoibhneas Womens Refuge
Ballymun
Dublin 11
Ph: 01-8422377

AONTAS National Association of
Adult Education
22 Earlsfort Terrece
Dublin 2
Ph: 01-4754121/4754122

Association for the Rights of Separated
Spouses
65 Meadow Mount
Dundrum
Dublin 14

Association of Secondary School
Teachers
Winetavern St
Dublin 8
Ph: 01-6719144

Association of Teachers of Home Economics
40 Annadale Drice
Dublin 9

Aware
147 Phibsboro Rd
Dublin 7
Ph: 01-6791711 (helpline)
Aware has branches nationwide, write for details.

B

Baha's Womens Group
24 Burlinton Road
Dublin 4
Ph: 01-6683150
Fax: 01-6689632

Ballyboden Family Resource Centre
29 Whitechurch Way
Ballyboden
Dublin 16
Ph: 01-4935953

Banulacht Women in Development
c/o Nat Youth Federation
20 Lr. Dominick St
Dublin 1
Ph: 01-8726952
Fax: 01-8724183

Business and Professional Womens Clubs
Carrick
42 Upper Newcastle
Galway

C

Catholic Womens Federation
18 Fitzwilliam Square
Dublin 2

Centre for Counselling & Psychotherapy
7 Father St
Cork
Ph: 021-968086

Centre for Creative Change
Psychotherapy Counselling
14 Upper Clanbrassil St
Dublin 8
Ph: 01-4538356

CHALLENGE
Silchester House
Glenageary
Co Dublin
Ph: 01-2801624

Cherish (Assoc. of Single Mothers)
2 Lower Pembroke St
Dublin 2
Ph: 01-6682744

Christian Feminist Movement
58 St Jarlaths Road
Cabra
Dublin 7

Civil & Public Service Union
Womens Committee
72 Lower Leeson Street
Dublin 2
Ph: 01-6765394
Fax: 01-6762918

CLLC
7/8 St Augustine Street
Cork
Ph: 021-271087

Clondalkin Womens Network
1A Castle Crescent
Monastery Road
Clondalkin
Dublin
Ph: 01-4595661
Fax: 01-4593262

Clonmel Rape Crisis Centre
20 Mary Street
Clonmel
Co Tipperary
Ph: 052-27677

Comfort for Cancer
5 Summerhill Road
Sandycove
Co Dublin
Ph: 01-2806505

Comhlamh Womens Group
55 Grand Parade
Cork
Ph: 021-275881
Fax: 021-275881

Council for the Status of People with Disabilities
21 Hill Street
Dublin 1
Ph: 01-8745213

Cork Womens Poetry Circle
Art Hive
McCurtain Street
Cork
Ph: 021-509274

Cork Womens Political Association
Allendale
19 Ballincurrig Park
Douglas Road, Cork

Creative Counselling Centre
82 Upper Georges Street
Dunloghaire
Co Dublin
Ph: 01-2802523

Creative Self Healing
Ph: 01-2854807

D

DES
c/o NWCI
32 Upper Fitzwilliam Street
Dublin 2
Ph: 01-6615268
Fax: 01-6760860

Divorce Action Group
54 Mid Abbey Street
Dublin 1
Ph: 01-8727395

E

Ecumenical Forum of European Christian Women
Convent of Mercy
Naas
Co Kildare
Ph: 045-897673

Enniscorthy Women's Group
The Moyne
Enniscorthy, Co Wexford

F

Family Life Service
12 Roches Road
Wexford
Ph: 053-23086

Fingal Centre for the Unemployed
7 Main Street
Finglas
Dublin 11
Ph: 01-8641970

First Out
c/o LOT
5-6 Capel Street
Dublin 1
Ph: 01-8727770

G

Galway Association of Women Graduates
The Sycamores
Revagh Road
Rockbarton
Galway

General Practitioners' Wives Association
c/o IMO House
107 Clonskeagh Road
Dublin 6
Ph: 01-2697788

Gingerbread
29/30 Dame Street
Dublin 2
Ph: 01-6710291

Girls Friendly Society
36 Upper Leeson Street
Dublin 4
Ph: 01-6603754

Graphic, Paper & Media Union
Graphic House
107 Clonskeagh Road
Dublin 6
Ph: 01-2697788
Fax: 01-2839977

H

HEALTH BOARDS
Eastern Health Board
Dublin
Ph: 01-6970700
Kildare
Ph: 045-76001
Wicklow
Ph: 0404-68400

Midland Health Board
Limerick, Clare, Tipperary
Ph: 061-316655

North Eastern Health Board
Cavan, Louth, Meath and Monaghan
Ph: 046-40341

North Western Health Board
Donegal, Sligo, Leitrim
Ph: 072-55123

South Eastern Health Board
Carlow, Kilkenny, Tipperary, South Riding, Waterford and Wexford
Ph: 056-21702

Southern Health Board
Cork and Kerry
Ph: 021-545011

Home Birth Centre of Ireland
25 Larkfield Grove
Terenure
Dublin 6W
Ph: 01-4922565

I

I.S.P.C.C.
Central Office
20 Molesworth St
Dublin 2
Ph: 01-6794944

Irish Agricultural Advisors
Liberty Hall
Dublin

Irish Association of Autistic Children
16 Lower O'Connell Street
Dublin 1
Ph: 01-8744684

Irish Association of Dental Surgery Assistants
10 Norton Avenue
Dublin 7

Irish Association of Eating Disorders
Progress House
47 Harrington Street
Dublin 8
Ph: 01-4975667

Irish Association of Humanistic & Integrative Psychotherapy
82 Upper Georges Street

Dunlaoghaire
Co Dublin
Ph: 01-2841665

Irish Association of Social Workers
114-116 Pearse Street
Dublin 2
Ph: 01-6771930
Fax: 01-6715734

Irish Association of Victim Support
Tallaght Branch
Main Street
Dublin 1
Ph: 01-4599511

Irish Childbirth Trust
82 Earlwood Estate
The Lough
Cork
Ph: 021-968202

Irish Countrywomen's Association
58 Merrion Road
Dublin 4
Ph: 01-6680453
Fax: 01-6609423

Irish Family Planning Association
Halfpenny Court
36/37 Lower Ormond Quay
Dublin 1
Ph: 01-8725033
Fax: 01-8726639

Irish Farmers Association
Farm Family Committee
Irish Farm Centre
Bluebell
Dublin 12
Ph: 01-4501166
Fax: 01-551043

Irish Federation of University Teachers
11 Merrion Square
Dublin 2
Ph: 01-6610910/6610909
Fax: 01-6610909

Irish Federation of University Women
7 Hollwood Park
Goatstown
Co Dublin

Irish Feminist Information
29 Upper Mount Street
Dublin 2
Ph: 01-6616128
Fax: 01-6616176

Irish Nurses Organisation
11 Fitzwilliam Place
Dublin 2
Ph: 01-6760137

Irish Nutrition & Diebetic Association
17 Rathfarnham Road
Dublin 6W
Ph: 01-4903237

Irish Psychoanalytical Association
2 Belgrave Terrece
Monkstown
Co Dublin
Ph: 01-2801869

Irish School of Acupressure
Dun Mhuire
Greenfield Road
Sutton
Dublin 13

Irish Stillbirth & Neo-Natal Death Society
Dublin
Ph: 01-2957785

Irish Sudden Infant Death Association
4 North Brunswick Street
Dublin 7
Ph: 1800-391391 (freephone)

J

Judith Ashton
Psychotherapist and Massage, Body and Self Awareness Tutor
Cappa Farm
Inistioge
Co Kilkenny
Ph: 056-58722

Judith Crowe
Counselling and Self Development
Childbirth Preparation and Support
The Hermitage
Newtownmountkennedy
Co Wicklow
Ph: 01-2819515

K

Kilkenny Womens Studies Group
c/o Adult Education Office
Ormond Road
Kilkenny

L

La Leche League, Brestfeeding Information
52 Clonard Drive
Dublin 16
Ph: 01-2955451

L

Legal Aid Board
(Law Centre)
Cork
Ph: 021-275998/300365

Lesbian Equality Networks
5/6 Capel Street
Dublin 1
Ph: 01-8727770

Lesbian Line
Cork.
(Thurs-8pm-10pm)
Ph: 021-271087

Lesbian Line
Carmichael House
Brunswick Street North
Dublin 7
Ph: 01-8729911

Letterkenny's Women Centre Ltd
Port Road
Letterkenny
Co Donegal
Ph: 074-24985

M

Menston
Westfield Park
Bray
Co Wicklow
Ph: 01-2829804
and
5 The Crescent
Dunshaughlin
Co Meath
Ph: 01-8258087

Magdalen Bristow
Women's Health Issues
Workshop Tutor and Lecturer
Ph: (01) 284 2342

Mandate
O'Lehane House
9 Cavendish Row
Dublin 1
Ph: 01-8746321/8746634

Manufacturing Science and Finance Union
Womens Committee
15 Merrion Square, Dublin 2
Ph: 01-6611063

Marriage Counselling Service Ltd
24 Grafton Street
Dublin 2
Non-Denominational Counselling
Ph: 01-8720341

Mater Hospital
Eccles Street
Dublin 7
Ph: 01-8301122

Miscarriage Association of Ireland
Fernhurst
Fennells Bay
Myrtleville
Co Cork

Mothers Union
Music Room/Christ Church Cathedral
Dublin 8
Ph: 01-6712475

Muintir-na-Tire
Canon Hayes House
Tipperary
Ph: 062-51163

N

N.A.T.O.
35 Meath Place
Dublin 8
Ph: 01-4543842

Naas Womens Group
3 Lakeside Park
Naas
Co Kildare

National Adult Literacy Agency
76 Lower Gardiner Street
Dublin 1
Ph: 01-8554332

National Association for the Deaf
35 North Frederick Street
Dublin 1
Ph: 01-8723800

National Childline
Freephone 1800-666-666

National Childrens Nursery Association
Nippers Nursery
Ash Grove
Navan Road
Castleknock
Dublin 15
Ph: 01-8212553

National Council for the Blind
21a Lower Dorset Street
Dublin 9
Ph: 01-8745421

National Council for the Elderly
22 Merrion Square
Dublin 2
Ph: 01-6765499

National Council for Travelling People
12 Westmoreland Street
Dublin 2

National Drugs Advisory Board
63 Adelaide Road
Dublin 2
Ph: 01-6764971

National Pregnancy Helpline
Ph: 0850-495051

National Women's Council of Ireland
64 Lower Mount Street
Dublin 2
Ph: 01-6607731

New Opportunities for Women
Contact: Mary Donnelly
Programme Manager
National Women's Council of Ireland
Ph: 01-6615268

O

Ombudsman
52 Stephens Green
Dublin 2
Ph: 01-6785222

OMEP(Ireland)
PO Box 2227
Dublin 1

One Parent Exchange & Network
c/o PARC
Bunratty Drive
Coolock
Dublin 17
Ph: 01-8484811

Openline Counselling
13 Marlborough Road
Donnybrook
Dublin 4
Ph: 01-6680043

Overeaters Anonymous
PO Box 2529
Dublin 5
Ph: 01-4515138

P

P.A.T.C.H. Information Services
20 Mark Street
Tullamore
Co Offaly
Freephone 1800-323232

Parents Alone Resource Centre
Community Project
Bunratty Drive
Dublin 17
Ph: 01-8481116

Parkinsons Association of Ireland
Carmichael House
North Brunswick Street
Dublin 7
Ph: 01-8722234

Parlaimint na mBan
7 Cearnog Mhuirfen
Atha Cliath 2
Ph: 01-6763222

Pavee Point Action & Development Group
Travelling Travellers Centre
Pavee Point
46 North Gate
Charles Street

Dublin 1
Ph: 01-8732802

Post Natal Distress Association of Ireland
11 Macken Street
Dublin 2

Presbyterian Womens Association
45 Stillorgan Park
Blackrock
Co Dublin

Public Service Executive Union
30 Merrion Square
Dublin 2
Ph: 01-6767271/2

R

Rape Crisis Centre
Mary Street
Clonmel
Ph: 052-27677
Freephone 1800-340340

Rape Crisis Centre
3 St Augustine Street
Galway
Ph:091-564983

Rape Crisis Centre
1st Floor
11 Denny Street
Tralee
Co Kerry
Ph: 066-23122

Rape Crisis Centre
2nd Floor
17 Upper Mallow Street
Limerick
Ph: 061-311511

Rape Crisis Centre
33 Georges Street
Waterford
Ph: 051-73362

Rape Crisis Service
Cork
Ph: 021-968086

Reach for Recovery
5 Northumberland Road
Dublin
Ph: 01-6681855

Redwood Ireland Training Association
Assertiveness, Personal Development,
Sexuality
Annamoe
Bray
Co Wicklow
Ph: 01-4044525/6602100

Refuge for Abused Women
Cork
Ph: 021-277698

Dublin
Ph: 01-8422377

Galway
Ph: 091-65985

Waterford
Ph: 051-70367

Meath
Ph: 046-22393

Westmeath
Ph: 0902-74249

Wicklow
Contact Merriall Kidd
c/o Health Centre

Strand Road
Bray
Co Wicklow

Rosemary Khalifa
Holistic Healer and Massage
Ph: 01-8330656

Rowlagh Womens Group Ltd
Rowlagh Health Centre
Collinstown Road
Clondalkin
Dublin 22

S

Samaritans, The
112 Marlborough Street
Dublin 1
Ph: 01-8727700
Callsave 1850-609090

Separated Persons Association
67 Blessington Street
Dublin 1
Ph: 01-8381101

Sexual Assualt Unit
Rotunda Hospital
Parnell Square
Dublin
Ph: 01-8730700

Shanty Educational Project
The Shanty
Glenaraneen
Brittas
Co Dublin
Ph: 01-4582194

Sligo Womens Group
The Manse
Wine Street, Sligo

Social Services Centre
Day Centre
Pearse Street
Dublin 2
Ph: 01-6773253

Soroptimist International
Ardlea
Newtown Road
Wexford
Ph: 071-60646

STEM
6 Priory Lawn
Ballybeg
Waterford

Support & Advice for Women
51 Dromheath Drive
Ladyswell
Dublin 15

Support Organisation for Tristomy
6 Emerald Cottages
Grand Canal Street
Ballsbridge
Dublin 4

T

Tallaght Womens Contact Centre
2 College View
Main Street
Tallaght
Dublin 24
Ph: 01-4524883

Teachers Union of Ireland
73 Orwell Road
Rathgar

Dublin 6
Ph: 01-4922588

Think Bodywhys Limited
Eating Disorder Support
c/o 17 Yale
Ardilea
Clonskeagh
Dublin 14

Tralee Womens Forum
43/44 Ashe Street
Tralee
Co Kerry
Ph: 066-20054

U

UCD Womens Graduates Association
Public Affairs Office
UCD, Belfield
Dublin 4
Ph: 01-7061713

Union of Students in Ireland
1-2 Aston Place
Temple Bar
Dublin 2
Ph: 01-6710088

V

Victoria Hospital
Sexually Transmitted Disease
Public Clinics
Cork
Ph: 021-968086

W

Waterford Womens Federation
4 Blenheim Heights
Waterford

Well Woman Centre
73 Lower Leeson Street
Dublin 2
Ph: 01-6610083

Western Womens Link
Eglinton House
34 Lower Dominick Street
Galway
Ph: 091-68974

Women and AIDS
PO Box 1884
Sheriff Street
Dublin 1
Ph: 01-6710895

Women Artists Action Group
23/25 Moss Street
Dublin 2

Women in Golf
12 Ardlieu Park
Blackrock
Co Dublin

Women in Learning
305 Clontarf Road
Dublin 3

Women in Technology and Science
PO Box 3783
Dublin 4

Women in the Home
12 Springfield Road
Dublin 6W
Ph: 01-8212012

Women in the Media and Entertainment
10 St Brigids Place Lower
Dublin 2
Ph: 01-6711687

Women of the North West
Ballyduane
Kincon
Ballina
Co Mayo
Ph: 096-31900

Womens Information Network
53 Parnell Square
Dublin 1
Ph: 01-4599511

Womens Aid
PO Box 791
Dublin 1
Ph: 01-8745302
Freephone: 1800-341900

Womens Education Research and Resource Centre
Room F104B
Arts Building
UCD
Dublin 4
Ph: 01-7068571

Womens Political Association
2 Erne Terrace, rear
off Upper Erne Street
Dublin 2

Womens Refuge
Adapt House
Rosbrien
Limerick
Ph: 061-412354

Womens Studies Centre
UCG
Baile na Coiribe
Galway
Ph: 091 -524411

YWCA of Ireland
49 St Johns Road
Sandymount
Dublin 4
Ph: 01-2692205

Y

Youth Information Centre
Blanchardstown Main Street
Dublin 24
Ph: 01-8212102

These leaflets, pamphlets and booklets may be obtained from the Healt Promotion Unit, Hawkins House, Dublin 2. Tel: 01-6714711, free of charge.

ALCOHOL
Women and Alcohol
You, Drink and Your Children
You, Drink and Your Life
You, Drink and Young People

BABIES AND CHILDREN
Book of the Child
Food & Babies (being reprinted, available in Autumn)
Gastroenteritis
Headlice
Meningitis
Prevention of Neural Tube Defects
Play it Safe
Protect your Child Immunise
Reduce the Risks of Cot Death
Screening for Metabolic Disorders
Toxoplasmosis

DRUGS/SOLVENT ABUSE
Cannibis
Drugs your Choice your Life (For Young People)
Ecstacy
Solvent Abuse (A guide for Parents and Professionals only)
Understanding Drugs (For Parents)

GENERAL
AIDS — The Facts
Backcare
Diabetes — The Facts
Eating Disorders (Anorexia and Bullimia Nervosa)
Family Planning and Contraception
Footcare
General Health Information for People Travelling Abroad
Hepatitis B The Other Virus
Influenza
Listeria and Listeriosis
Sexually Transmissible Diseases
The Aging Foot
The Sun Seekers Guide to Health

HYGIENE
At Home with Food Hygiene
Get Mr Germ On The Run

NUTRITION
Be a Healthy Weight (A5)
Be a Healthy Weight (A4)
Healthy Food Choices
Healthy Food Magazine
Your Childs Lunchbox

POSTERS
AIDS
Alcohol
Anti-Smoking Stickers and Signs
CPR (Save a Life)
Drugs
First Aid Index Chart
Nutrition

WOMENS HEALTH
Cystitis
Hysterectomy
Menopause
Periods
The Gynae Book